THE EDUCATION OF KARL WITTE

OR

THE TRAINING OF THE CHILD

EDITED, WITH AN INTRODUCTION, BY

H. ADDINGTON BRUCE

TRANSLATED FROM THE GERMAN BY

LEO WIENER

PROFESSOR OF SLAVIC LANGUAGES IN HARVARD UNIVERSITY

NEW YORK

THOMAS Y. CROWELL COMPANY

PUBLISHERS

Published March, 1914.

CONTENTS

EDITOR'S INTRODUCTION

WHEN, less than six months ago, I suggested in the course of an article contributed to *The Outlook,* the great desirability of an English translation of that remarkable book, "Karl Witte: Oder Erziehungs- und Bildungsgeschichte Desselben. Ein Buch für Eltern und Erziehende," I had no idea that the opportunity would so soon be afforded of assisting to carry out this suggestion myself. There are few tasks I have undertaken that have appealed to me so strongly, for the reason that Pastor Witte's account of the early home training of his son must unquestionably be regarded as one of the most inspiring and helpful contributions ever made to the literature of education. I say this with full appreciation of the fact that nearly a hundred years have passed since it was written, and that in the meantime it has dropped so completely out of sight that few even among the most erudite exponents of the modern "science of pedagogy" have any acquaintance with it. In fact, so far as I am aware, and I have made diligent inquiry, the copy from which this first translation into English has been made—and which I found reposing long undisturbed in the Treasure Room of Harvard University Library—is the only copy in the United States.

There are two reasons for Witte's book having thus fallen into temporary oblivion. In its original form it is a book which, to employ the quaint but extremely expressive German phrase, "does not allow itself to be read." Not only is it excessively long, running to more than a thousand pages of print, but it is burdened with a mass of disquisitional passages which too often are of little importance, and which, in addition to exhausting the reader's patience, have the effect of diminishing his appreciation of the value of the educational method which Witte laboriously and disconnectedly details. Consequently it has been a necessary task, in connection with the present translation, to eliminate as far as possible the superfluous and beclouding material, while at the same time endeavoring to omit nothing really essential to an understanding of the principles guiding Witte in the education of his son. But even had it not been weighted down by a heavy handicap of form and style, his book was foredoomed to be left for many years unread and unheeded because of the impossibility of reconciling its teachings with the "established" educational doctrines of the age.

Witte's fundamental principle—that the education of a child should begin with the dawning of the child's intelligence—came into direct collision with the accepted pedagogical policy of refraining from anything in the way of formal education until the child reached "school age." By beginning too soon to teach and train a child, the prevalent theory ran, not only will the child be robbed of the joys of childhood but there will also be grave danger of seriously, perhaps irreparably, injuring his health by overstraining his mind. It was in vain that Witte could and did point to the success of his daring experiment in the upbringing of his own child. The outcome of that experiment, in the opinion of most educational authorities, proved, not the wisdom of the course followed, but the exceptional innate ability of the child on whom the experiment was made.

This insistence on the propriety of allowing the mind of the very young child to "lie fallow" has continued to be the dominant feature in pedagogical thought to the present day. The inevitable result, especially in countries having a highly developed public school system, has been to throw virtually the whole burden of education on the schools. And not until recent years has there been any real appreciation of the fact that the schools are not able to carry it. To-day, however, in addition to widespread and not altogether helpful denunciation of the "breakdown of the public school system," educators are seriously beginning to ask themselves if too much has not been expected of the schools; if their "failure to develop really rational men and women"[1] is not in great part due to the unworkability of the material—the boys and girls of the nation—with which the schools have to deal; and if this unworkability in its turn may not chiefly be the result of neglecting to begin

[1]As charged, for example, in Dr Charles W. Eliot's declaration: "Our common schools have failed signally to cultivate general intelligence, as is evinced by the failure to deal adequately with the liquor problem, by the prevalence of gambling, of strikes accompanied by violence, and by the persistency of the spoils system."

the process of education in the home before the boys and girls are old enough to be sent to school.

In support of this new view stress is laid on certain results of recent scientific research; results going to show, for example, that early impressions are the most lasting, that early childhood is undoubtedly the time when habits good or bad are most readily formed, and that neglect of a child's mentality in early life may mean lifelong mental inferiority. In fact, notwithstanding the orthodox pedagogical dread of infantile overstrain, scientific students of the nature and characteristics of man are beginning boldly to assert that the sooner a child's education is begun the better it will be for that child. As one able investigator, Dr. T. A. Williams, of Washington, has recently put it:

> An impression prevails that growing organs should not be subjected to work. This is a gross error; for organs which do not work cannot grow well. Even the bones become tough, hard, and large in proportion to the stresses to which they are subjected by frequent and vigorous pulls where the muscles are attached. . . . What is true of structure is true of functional power. From ballet dancers to violin virtuosi, artists must be trained from early youth. It may be objected that this

is because muscular agility is required, but this objection is only superficial; for dexterity of an artist is made possible, not in virtue of superior coordinations of movements themselves, but by means of the superior speed and accuracy of the guiding mental processes which reside in the brain. Since intellectual activity is also a result of orderly functioning of mental processes seated in the brain, it should be manifest that these too should reach excellence best when they are trained by a capable hand during the formative period of early youth. This *a priori* assumption I believe to be borne out by experience.[1]

Writing to the same effect, another brilliant American medical psychologist, Dr. Boris Sidis, unhesitatingly affirms that in the case of the vast majority of children the proper time for beginning their education is in the second or third year of life. He adds:

It is at that time that the child begins to form his interests. It is at that critical period that we have to seize the opportunity to guide the child's formative energies in the right channels. To delay is a mistake and a wrong to the child. We can at that early period awaken a love of knowledge which will persist through life. The child will as eagerly play in the game of knowledge as he now spends the most of his energies in meaningless games and objectless silly sports.

We claim we are afraid to force the child's mind. We claim we are afraid *to strain his brain prematurely*. This is an error. In *directing* the *course* of the use of the child's energies we do not force the child. If we do

[1] In *The Pedagogical Seminary*, Vol XVIII, p 85.

not *direct* the energies in the right course, the child will *waste* them in the *wrong* direction. . . . In my practice as physician in nervous and mental diseases, I can say without hesitation that I have not met a single case of nervous or mental trouble caused by too much thinking or overstudy. This is now the opinion of the best psychopathologists. What produces nervousness is worry, emotional excitement, and lack of interest in the work. But that is precisely what we do with our children. We do not take care to develop a love of knowledge in their early life for fear of brain injury, and then when it is late to acquire the interest we force them to study, and we cram them and feed them and stuff them like geese. What you often get is fatty degeneration of the mental liver.

If, however, you do not neglect the child between the second and third year, and see to it that the brain should not be starved, should have its proper function, like the rest of the bodily organs, by developing an interest in intellectual activity and love of knowledge, no forcing of the child to study is afterward requisite. The child will go on by himself,—he will derive intense enjoyment from his intellectual activity, as he does from his games and physical exercise. The child will be stronger, healthier, sturdier than the present average child, with its purely animal activities and total neglect of brain-function. His physical and mental development will go apace. He will not be a barbarian with animal proclivities and a strong distaste for knowledge and mental enjoyment, but he will be a strong, healthy, thinking man.[1]

[1] In "Philistine and Genius," pp 67-68, 84-86, Moffat, Yard & Co., New York, 1911. The italics in the passages quoted are Dr. Sidis's.

Now, this is the very position that was taken by Karl Witte a hundred years ago. In an age when no enlightenment was possible to him from anthropology, psychology, and the allied modern sciences that have for their chief object the study of human characteristics; in an age when tradition and dogma still enslaved pedagogical theory, this humble country clergyman in a little German village arrived by some miraculous power of intuition at the selfsame conclusions held by the most advanced educational thinkers of the present day. Surely it is not surprising, on the one hand, that his book made no impression on the people of his own generation; and on the other hand that, after having lain so long unnoticed, it now challenges attention in the light of the increasing recognition that the education of the schoolroom must be supplemented and preceded by the education of the home. My own belief is that it offers to parents precisely the information and guidance indispensable to the proper performance of this all-important task.

Certainly the educational method adopted by Witte is so simple that it can be utilized by anybody; and certainly the results obtained in the case of his son are of a character that must appeal to every right-minded parent. Let me briefly review the facts, as set forth partly in the present volume and partly in the son's career subsequent to the writing of his father's account of his education.

The elder Witte, as has just been said, was a clergyman in a German village, a man of simple habits but of uncommonly original and forceful ways of thinking. Looking at the world about him, he saw it peopled largely with men and women who wasted their energies in all sorts of dissipation. As a moralist he was saddened and depressed by the drunkenness, gambling, sexual irregularities, that he found everywhere. Still more he marveled that such things could be, among rational human beings.

"These poor people," he reflected, "do not reason, do not use their God-given intellects. If they did they would spend their lives altogether differently, and would devote themselves to things of true worth. The trouble must be that they have not been educated aright. They have not been taught how to think and what to think about. They have been started wrong in life. The schools and universities are to blame, but their parents are far more to blame. If love of the good, the beautiful, and the true had been implanted properly in them in early youth, if they had been trained from the first really to use their minds, they would not now be living so foolishly."

Holding such views, Witte carefully mapped out a program which he proceeded to follow in the upbringing of his son Karl, who was born in July of the year 1800. As its foundation it had the theory that since children are essentially thinking animals they are certain, from the moment they first use their minds, to draw inferences and arrive at conclusions regarding everything they see, hear, and touch; but if left to themselves will inevitably, because of their inability unaided to form sound critical judgments, acquire wrong interests and thought habits which all the education of later life may not be able wholly to overcome. It was Witte's great aim, therefore, to direct and develop his son's reasoning powers in the plastic, formative years of childhood—to "start him thinking right."

He began, even before the little fellow

could speak, by naming to him different parts of the human body, the objects in his bedroom, etc. As the boy grew older, so that he could toddle up and down stairs and walk with his father through their garden and in the streets and fields of his native village of Lochau, Witte gradually widened the horizon of his knowledge, giving him ever more information about matters of practical utility or æsthetic worth.

He encouraged the child to ask questions, and in his replies went as fully as he could into the whys and wherefores of whatever was under discussion. Above all things he avoided giving superficial answers, for it was his chief object to impress upon Karl the desirability of thoroughness, the importance of reasoning closely and carefully, of appreciating analogies, dissimilarities, relationships, and also of being able to reason logically from cause to effect. Nor in their daily walks and conversations did he make any attempt to "talk down" to his son, as so many parents are wont to do. "Baby talk" had no place in his program. Since language is the tool of thought, he argued, every child should be taught as soon as possible to express itself in its mother tongue, clearly, fluently, purely. Not the least important element in Karl's education, in his father's opinion, was the systematic drilling he received in the correct pronunciation of letters and words, and in the correct use of the different parts of speech. His father insisted, too, that all others who talked with the child—his mother, the maid of all work, family visitors—should be careful how they spoke in his presence.

Under this system of intensive child culture Karl soon displayed not only a remarkable degree of intelligence but also a love of knowledge rarely seen in boys of any age. Before he was seven all who knew him were dumfounded at the proofs he gave of the great extent to which he had profited from his early training. Most impressive were his logical habits of mind, the fullness and accuracy of the information he even then possessed on a number of subjects, and his linguistic proficiency.

His study of foreign languages began with French, which his father taught him in a novel way, fully described in the chapter on his education in the languages. So successful was this special method that within a year

Karl was reading French with ease. Meanwhile he had begun the study of Italian, and from Italian passed to Latin. English came next, then the study of Greek, a language concerning which the boy's curiosity was whetted by tales from Homer and Xenophon told to him by his father. In every case the process was chiefly one of self-education, the father answering—when he could—the questions put to him by Karl, but always insisting that the proper way to learn anything is to overcome its difficulties for oneself. In all five languages the boy made such progress that by the time he was nine, according to his father's statement, he had read Homer, Plutarch, Virgil, Cicero, Ossian, Fénelon, Florian, and Metastasio, besides Schiller and other German writers.

Naturally his fame spread far and wide, and with its spreading much sharp criticism of his father was heard. He was accused of fanatically endeavoring to convert the child into a weird thinking machine, and of endangering his health and sanity. Karl himself was pictured as a pale, anemic, goggle-eyed "freak," who was vastly to be pitied. In reality he was a happy, joyous youngster, stıong of body and mind, as is impressively testified in the letter from the philologist Heyne to the philosopher and poet Wieland, printed on a later page. It was with reason that, in answering his critics, Witte indignantly denied Karl's alleged ill-health; and justly, too, he disclaimed the prodigy-making ambitions attributed to himself. All that he wished to do, as he explicitly states in his book, was to make sure that his son would enter adult life with well-trained mental as well as physical powers; if he thus early displayed marked intellectual ability, this was in itself proof of the great advantages to be gained by beginning education almost at the outset of existence.

Nor were Karl's studies as a little boy confined to the languages and literature. Aiming to make of him a well-rounded man, his father strove earnestly to awaken in him a love of art and science. Neither artist nor scientist himself, he none the less believed firmly that if he could only interest his son sufficiently in artistic and scientific subjects he would study them enthusiastically of his own accord. To this end he adopted the plan of taking Karl with him whenever he journeyed to Halle, Leipsic, or any other German city. There they would visit art galleries, natural history museums, zoological and botanical gardens, and all manner of manufacturing establishments, mines, shops, etc. Thus, under the guise of entertainment, Witte was able to impart to his son much elementary instruction in zoölogy, botany, physics, chemistry, etc. Always he emphasized the interrelationship of things, the importance of grasping first principles and of learning everything thoroughly.

And, in addition to these visits of exploration, he systematically utilized familiar, commonplace objects for the purposes of scientific education. He threw about them an attractive cloak of mystery, which piqued the boy's curiosity and made him eager to press forward to a solution. He also devised games through which he contrived to familiarize Karl with fundamental facts in various departments of knowledge. Always, however, he was careful to keep well in the background the educational purposes he had in view. To quote his own words:

"He would have been greatly surprised if told that he had been studying geography, physics, and so forth. I had carefully avoided the use of such terms, partly in order not to frighten him, and partly in order not to make him vain."

By the age of nine, in fact, Karl had learned so much, and was so well trained in the use of his mental powers, that his father determined to send him to college. Six months later, accordingly, the boy matriculated at Leipsic University, to begin a scholastic career of marvelous achievement. It is not necessary here to give details of it, as a full account will be found in the closing chapter. Enough to say that in 1814, before he had passed his fourteenth birthday, he was granted the Ph.D. distinction, and two years later, at the age of sixteen, was made a Doctor of Laws, being also appointed to the teaching staff of the University of Berlin!

Instead, however, of immediately beginning professorial duties, Karl, with the aid of no less a personage than the King of Prussia, now spent a few years in foreign travel, and it was during a sojourn in Italy that an event occurred which had an important bearing on his after-life. In Florence, where he resided for some time, he chanced to make the acquaintance of a talented woman, who, speaking one day of the masters of Italian literature, said to him, half in jest and half in earnest:

"There is one Italian writer, the greatest of all, whose books I should advise you to let alone. We Italians sometimes try to persuade ourselves that we understand Dante, but we do not. If a foreigner sets about it, we can scarcely repress a smile."

One of Karl's first acts after this extraordinary speech was to buy an elaborate edition of the "Divine Comedy." Reading it thoughtfully, he next read what the commentators had to say about it, and was at once impressed with what he considered the narrowness, thinness, and downright error of their views. Fascinated by the magic of the great word-painter's verse, he promised himself that some day he would institute a campaign for the better appreciation of Dante; and this promise he fulfilled five years later by the publication, in Germany, of one of the most important literary essays of the nineteenth century. It was entitled "On Misunderstanding Dante," and concerning it a modern authority on the study of Dante, Mr. Philip H. Wicksteed, in an introduction to a translation of Witte's "Essays on Dante," has this to say:

> If the history of the revival of interest in Dante which has characterized this century should ever be written, Karl Witte would be the chief hero of the tale. He was little more than a boy when, in 1823, he entered the lists against existing Dante scholars, all and sundry, demonstrated that there was not one of them that knew his task, and announced his readiness to teach it to them. The amazing thing is that he fully accomplished his vaunt. His essay exercised a growing influence in Germany, and then in Europe; and after five-and-forty years of indefatigable and fruitful toil, he was able to look back upon his youthful attempt as containing the germ of all his subsequent work on Dante. But now, instead of the audacious young heretic and revolutionist, he was the acknowledged master of the most prominent Dante scholars in Germany, Switzerland, Italy, England, and America.

In fact, as I stated in my *Outlook* article,[1] "The Story of Karl Witte," of which this summary of his career is an abridgment, there came from Witte's pen, almost to the time of his death, a steady succession of essays, commentaries, and translations, to serve as a continual stimulus to an ever-widening circle of Dante scholars. Yet all the while the propagation of his views on Dante, and the foster-

[1] *The Outlook*, Vol. C, pp 211-218.

ing of a love for Dante, were but incidental to Witte's real life-work. That was the teaching of the principles of law, both in the classroom and by the pen. It was in 1821, shortly after his return from abroad, that he was established as a lecturer on jurisprudence at the University of Breslau, being appointed to a full professorship two years later—at the age of twenty-three!—and being transferred to Halle in 1834. There, teaching and writing and gaining ever greater renown, he passed the remainder of his life.

Long before he died, honored and lamented, in his eighty-third year, every one of the wiseacres who had so confidently prophesied a short and unhappy existence for him, had preceded him to the grave. Still further to confound their dire predictions, he retained to the last his great mental powers; and to the last he fondly cherished the memory of the father who had so carefully planned and so faithfully carried out his early education.

Such in rough outline is the record of Karl Witte's intellectual training and achievement. Did it stand by itself it might plausibly be argued, as the contemporaries of the elder Witte argued, that in the last analysis the essential thing was not the training given by the father but the possession of extraordinary native talent by the son. But the interesting fact remains to be noted that Witte's experiment does not stand alone. Since his time—in some instances, I do not doubt, as a direct result of the reading of his book—it has been repeated by a number of other parents, and always with a similar result.

The children thus trained from infancy have not broken down in bodily or mental health; on the contrary they have been if anything stronger of physique than the average child, while mentally they have, like Karl Witte, developed and retained powers incomparably superior to those of the average child. When this uniformity of result is taken into account; when it is pondered in the light of the findings of modern psychology with respect to the formative influences of environment, habit, suggestion, etc.; when regard is had to the demonstrated inability of the schools to attain the ends expected of them, it manifestly becomes imperative to acknowledge both the advisability and the wonderful developmental possibilities of education in the home and by the parent.

Compare, for example, the results obtained in the case of Karl Witte with those obtained by a certain James Thomson, who in the early part of last century was a mathematical master in a Belfast academy. Thomson, like Witte's father, and possibly in consequence of acquaintance with the latter's work, firmly believed in the importance of beginning a child's education in the first years of life, and had the courage of his convictions when blessed with children of his own. With the loyal coöperation of his wife, he taught them to spell and read almost as soon as they could utter words; he taught them mathematics, history, geography, and the elements of natural science. One of the busiest of men—a writer of mathematical text-books as well as a classroom instructor—he made great sacrifices for the sake of their education. He would even get up at four in the morning to work on his text-books and to prepare his lectures, so that he might be sure of having freedom to instruct his little ones during the day.

His two older sons, James and William, were the special objects of his care, particularly after their mother's death, which occurred when James was eight and William six. Thereafter he literally lived with these two boys, taking them to sleep in the same room with him, making them his companions in long walks, diligently drilling them in the rudiments of an all-round education. When he was eventually called from Belfast to assume the arduous tasks and more responsible position of professor of mathematics at Glasgow University, he continued the home education of his sons, besides securing permission for them, at the ages of ten and eight, to attend his university lectures and the lectures of some of the other professors.

In full agreement with his expectations, both boys showed an amazing mental development, while remaining healthy, vigorous, and active, full of fun and ever ready for a frolic. Like ordinary boys they delighted in playing with toys—with this difference, that their toys were in many instances scientific instruments. Thus, when barely nine years old, William made with his own hands little electrical machines and Leyden jars, wherewith to give harmless and laughter-provoking shocks to his playmates.

So great, indeed, were the intellectual attainments of the two brothers that when James was twelve and William ten they were admitted as regular students at the university. Nor, children though they were, did they have any difficulty in keeping up with their studies. On the contrary, throughout their college careers, and in several departments of knowledge, they stood at the very top of their classes. In his first winter's work, before he was eleven, William took two prizes in the "humanity" class. The next year he began the study of natural history and Greek, spent his Christmas vacation translating Lucian's "Dialogues of the Gods," and in May carried off the first prize for Greek. The year after that, as members of the junior mathematical class, he and his brother closed a brilliant session as first and second prizemen. Again they ranked first and second when members of the senior mathematical class; and, not content with this, William won an additional prize for proficiency in logic. The following year he won the class prize in astronomy, and a university medal for an essay, "On the Figure of the Earth," the manuscript of which is still in existence. He was then not sixteen, and among his classmates were men of twenty-five.

As in Karl Witte's time there were not

wanting prophets of evil, who, watching the achievements of the brothers, mournfully shook their heads. "It is monstrous, horrible, impossible," they protested. "These boys have been forced by their father beyond the limits of human endurance. No brain can stand it. They will die, or else they will go insane."

What actually happened? James Thomson, the older brother, lived to the age of seventy, and died leaving behind him the reputation of a really great authority on engineering. William, the younger, did not die until he was eighty-three, and became even more famous. For, as Lord Kelvin of Largs, greatest of nineteenth-century physicists, he won a place in the annals of science fairly comparable with that held by Newton, Faraday, or any other of the intellectual giants who have concededly done most to advance mankind in knowledge of nature's laws.

John Stuart Mill, the illustrious political economist, was similarly educated by a father who had strong convictions as to the importance of habituating a child to the purposeful exercise of his mind. Mill himself says:

I have no remembrance of the time when I began to learn Greek. I have been told that it was when I was three years old. My earliest recollection on the subject is that of committing to memory what my father termed vocables, being lists of common Greek words, with their signification in English, which he wrote out for me on cards. Of grammar until some years later I learned no more than the inflections of nouns and verbs, but after a course of vocables proceeded at once to translation; and I faintly remember going through "Æsop's Fables," the first Greek book which I read. The "Anabasis," which I remember better, was the second. I learned no Latin till my eighth year. At that time I had read, under my father's tuition, a number of Greek prose authors, among whom I remember the whole of Herodotus and of Xenophon's "Cyropædia" and "Memorials of Socrates"; some of the lives of the philosophers by Diogenes Laertius; part of Lucian, and "Isocrates ad Demonicum" and "Ad Nicoclem."[1]

It is safe to say that nine out of every ten readers of Mill's account of the educational process to which his father subjected him, have been moved to pity for the child and condemnation of the father. But Mill's after-life, especially when viewed in conjunction with Karl Witte's, Lord Kelvin's, and James Thomson's, assuredly vindicates his father's policy and emphasizes the unwisdom of the policy of mental neglect still in favor with most parents. The same, I have not the slightest doubt, may ultimately be said of the

[1] In John Stuart Mill's "Autobiography," Vol I, p. 5.

more recent experiments of our own time and country, in which several American fathers and mothers have, like the elder Mill and the elder Thomson, applied in the education of their children much the same method as that devised by Witte, and with results in the way of unusual intellectual attainment closely paralleling the results Witte obtained.

One of these latter-day educational innovators is the present translator of Witte's book, Professor Leo Wiener of Harvard University. Another is the psychologist, Dr. Boris Sidis, from whose writings I have already quoted, and whose insistence on the importance of early home training is an immediate outgrowth of his psychological researches. Dr. A. A. Berle, formerly pastor of Shawmut Congregational Church in Boston, now Professor of Applied Christianity in Tufts College, is a third; while a fourth is Mrs. J. B. Stoner, a resident of Pittsburgh. All four have acted on the theory that, if one only begins soon enough, it is just as easy to interest a child in things worth while as in activities which dissipate his energies and tend to the formation of loose and harmful habits of thought and conduct; and that study will never injure a child's mind as long as the child is really interested in what he is studying. They have therefore taken pains to give their children an environment rich in cultural suggestions, and have labored by precept and example to inspire in them a love for intellectual endeavor. In every case the children have responded to their efforts in an astonishing degree.

Professor Wiener's oldest boy, Norbert, developed such intellectual power in early childhood that he was able to enter Tufts College at ten, was graduated at fourteen, and, three months ago, at an age when most boys are only beginning their college careers, was granted the Ph.D. degree by Harvard University. Dr. Sidis's son, William, was admitted to the Brookline, Massachusetts, high school at eight, and three years ago, being even then a student in Harvard, amazed the members of that university's mathematical club by lecturing to them on the fourth dimension. Dr. Berle's daughter, Lina, matriculated into Radcliffe College at fifteen, while her younger brother, Adolf, passed the entrance examinations for Harvard when only thirteen and a half; both brother and sister have since completed their college courses with distinction, the boy in his sophomore year winning a prize for historical writing, and gaining his Bachelor degree in three years instead of the customary four. Finally, Mrs. Stoner's daughter, Winifred Sackville Stoner, at six was a frequent contributor to the poetry column of a newspaper in Evansville, Indiana, where she was then living with her parents; at seven published a volume of verse; and to-day, at eleven, besides being proficient in several languages, is writing a series of stories for a newspaper syndicate.

When it is added that the younger brothers and sisters of Norbert Wiener and of Lina and Adolf Berle have also been given the benefit of early home training along similar lines, and have similarly displayed exceptional mental ability, the difficulty of accounting for this result on the hypothesis of extraordinary innate talent becomes insuperable. As Dr. Berle, in discussing the education of his four children, has well said:

> If this result had been secured with one child, the usual plea of an "unusual child" might possibly be raised. But it is unthinkable that there should be four "prodigies" in one family! As a matter of fact, all such talk is

absurd. The difference is one of method, parental interest, and care.[1]

In not one case, moreover, can these American parents be justly accused of having "forced" their children, or of having by their educational methods done any injury to their children's health. The children are one and all healthy, sturdy, and strong, and each in his or her own way gets quite as much "fun" out of life as the ordinary child. I can say this from personal knowledge, for, with the exception of Mrs. Stoner's little daughter, all of them have been more or less under my observation for a number of years, and I have followed with interest the course of their development. Time alone, to be sure, can tell whether they will live to a good old age. But if they should die young or become insane, as some critics have dismally predicted, I am satisfied that neither misfortune could rightly be ascribed to their parents' treatment of them. My own opinion is that they have benefited physically as well as mentally from the way they have been brought up, and that

[1] In "The School in the Home," pp. 14-15 Moffat, Yard & Co., New York, 1912. Dr. Berle's book is a particularly helpful one to read in connection with Witte's.

they are altogether likely to do as Karl Witte did—outlive those who so confidently prophesy disaster for them.

But, it may be objected, the development of intellectual power is, after all, not the only end of education; the development of moral strength is even more important. Undoubtedly. And in this respect, readers of the present volume will very soon discover, the Wittean program for the upbringing of children is fully as helpful as with respect to their intellectual growth. For primarily, let me repeat, it was not Witte's object to make his son a "learned" man; what he wished to do was to make him an all-round man, strong morally as well as mentally and physically. If he believed that the boy's reasoning powers could not be properly developed unless he were trained from early infancy in the principles of sound reasoning, he was quite as firmly convinced that the process of moral development should likewise begin at the earliest possible moment. He believed this because he instinctively appreciated the force of a law on which scientific investigators are nowadays laying ever-increasing stress—the so-called law of psychological determinism.

Stated briefly, this law, with which all parents ought to be acquainted, holds that every occurrence in the moral life of a man is indissolubly connected with, and determined by, previous occurrences, and especially by the occurrences and influences of early childhood. Dr. Paul Dubois, one of the foremost exponents of the philosophy of determinism says:

If you have the happiness to be a well-living man, take care not to attribute the credit of it to yourself. Remember the favorable conditions in which you have lived, surrounded by relatives who loved you and set you a good example; do not forget the close friends who have taken you by the hand and led you away from the quagmires of evil; keep a grateful remembrance for all the teachers who have influenced you, the kind and intelligent schoolmaster, the devoted pastor; realize all these multiple influences which have made of you what you are. Then you will remember that such and such a culprit has not in his sad life met with these favorable conditions, that he had a drunken father or a foolish mother, and that he has lived without affection, exposed to all kinds of temptations. You will then take pity upon this disinherited man, whose mind has been nourished upon malformed mental images, begetting evil sentiments, such as immoderate desire or social hatred.[1]

In the case of the spoiled child, equally with that of the neglected one, the determinist

[1] In "Reason and Sentiment," pp 69-71 Funk & Wagnalls Co., New York, 1910.

sees the implanting of seeds certain soon or late to ripen into a harvest of moral weeds. And his cry, consequently, is for the beginning of moral education in the first years of childhood, so that by the time the child reaches school age he will have acquired a viewpoint and strength of character sufficient to enable him to resist the allurements of companions of perhaps vicious, or at all events morally weak, tendencies.

In such full agreement was Witte with this modern determinist doctrine of the supreme importance of the early environment as a factor in moral development, that he even laid down rules to be strictly observed by all in the household in their dealings with little Karl. The whole family life, in fact, was regulated with a view to "suggesting" to the child ideas which, taking root in the subconscious region of his mind, would tend to affect his moral outlook and exercise a lasting influence on his conduct. Hasty words, disputes, discussion of unpleasant topics, all such things were studiously avoided. From Witte's statements it is also plain that in their relations with one another, as with their serving-maid and all who visited their home,

Witte and his wife displayed only those characteristics with which they wished to imbue their son. They were unfailingly genial, courteous, considerate, and sympathetic. Over and above all this, they set Karl a constant example of diligence, of that earnest activity which is itself a most forceful form of moral discipline.

It is also worth noting that in the walks and talks which were so conspicuous a feature of Witte's educational program, he took good care to cultivate in his boy the precious gift of imagination, on which the moral as well as the mental life of man so largely depends.[1] When, for instance, father and son went hand in hand along the roads and across the fields of Lochau, it was not alone rudiments of botany, physics, chemistry, natural history, and the like, that Witte taught Karl; he deftly led him to appreciate the beauty and mystery inherent in the workings of na-

[1] This important measure in the education of the child is ably discussed in Dr Berle's book; also in Mr Ernest Hamlin Abbott's stimulating little volume, "On the Training of Parents." Houghton, Mifflin Co, Boston, 1908 In this connection it might also be said that parents will find much helpful advice on the subject of moral education in President William De Witt Hyde's "The Quest of the Best" Thomas Y. Crowell Co, New York, 1913

ture, led him to feel that there was always something beyond and transcending the outward actualities. When he told him stories of the ancient world, or showed him pictures of historic episodes, it was not simply with a view to interesting him in the study of history. The pathos, the grandeur, the tragedy, the heroism, or whatever it might be, exemplified in the particular story or picture, was also brought out clearly. So, likewise, in familiarizing him with the quiet life of Lochau itself, in introducing him to its mills, its shops, its cottage homes and their humble dwellers, Witte constantly endeavored to make his son perceive, beneath the sordid and petty and sometimes repellent externals, phases which, by appealing to his kindled imagination, would arouse sentiments of true sympathy.

"Remember, dear Karl," he would say, in effect, "these poor people have not had the advantages enjoyed by you. If they do not speak correctly, if they do not always behave as they ought, it is because they have not been taught properly in their youth. You must not do as they do, but neither must you condemn them. On the contrary, remember that they are God's children like yourself, and that in spite of their shortcomings they are precious to Him."

In short, by these and other measures which the reader will find described in his book, Witte sought to establish in his son those moral traits which the world unites in regarding as most desirable. His success is evinced by the nobility of that son's entire life—a life which, at its close, drew from one who knew Karl Witte well this impressive tribute:

"He lived in Halle for nearly fifty years, a loved man and honored teacher, a helpful and valued member of the professorial staff, a true patriot who had boldly stood at the head of the Prussenverein in the time of the Revolution, a loyal Conservative, a devout Christian and elder of the church, a scholar overwhelmed with honors and distinctions, a tender husband and father, till a gentle death closed his rich and singularly happy life on March 6, 1883."

So, too, the parents who have since Witte's day made trial of the virtues of early home training, have found their children growing in moral strength exactly in proportion as care has been taken to surround them, as

Witte did his son Karl, with enlightening and ennobling influences. Always the outcome is the same—the vindication of a method which cannot too soon be adopted by all parents.

Nor does this mean, as might be supposed, that in order to make sure of results, parents will have to give the greater portion of their time to their children's education. An hour or so a day is all that will be necessary in the way of formal instruction. What parents will have to do, however, is so to regulate their whole lives that the indirect, the unconscious instruction which their children will absorb from them will make for mental and moral betterment. Always they will have to bear firmly in mind that, as wise old Witte used to say, "Teaching begins, but example accomplishes."

H. ADDINGTON BRUCE.

MARLBORO, NEW HAMPSHIRE,
September, 1913

THE EDUCATION OF KARL WITTE

CHAPTER I

For Whom this Book is Written

PEOPLE may think that I am writing especially for teachers and educators proper, but that is not the case. Since the latter as a rule consider themselves, for good reasons or no reasons at all, to be my opponents, I cannot be writing for them in particular. Their objections to me are that I have not done things the way they do them,—which is bad enough,—and that at times I have done the very opposite from what they do,—which is much worse! Then, the public have been unkind enough to say: "If Witte did that with his son, and at the same time assures us that equally good results may be obtained in the case of every child not directly neglected by Nature, why do not our schoolmasters accomplish the same?" Nothing could be more unjust than this request, and I have made vain endeavors to stop it. Meanwhile the offensive accusations against the honest teachers make them impatient with me, who—truly against my will—am the cause of these accusations.

My whole work is intended to prove to the intelligent person that the schoolmaster, no matter how well endowed with knowledge and the ability to teach, is, in spite of his best wishes, unable to accomplish anything, if others have previously worked against him, or still continue to work against him.

Teachers and educators, for the above causes, are generally hostile toward me, at least so long as they have not become acquainted with me or have not in some way, from me or from others, learned of my convictions.

For these I write only in so far as they are also fathers and mothers who sincerely love their children, or the children entrusted to them, and out of their tender love for them have resolved to look closer at the educational experiment of a man who more than once has given them unpleasant moments.

If they do that, I shall be writing for them, as for all well-meaning parents who wish to get the best results for their children's bodies, minds, and souls. Many parents have attentively followed my methods of education, have in writing expressed their sympathy for me, or have treated me and mine with high favor. The proofs of their noble well-wishings have frequently touched me to tears. I may, nay, I must, say that they have often assisted me, as occasionally will appear in the course of my writing. My warm thanks and the thanks of my family will follow them to their graves.

I have been urgently asked by a great number of them to write in a simple manner, just as at their request I have been telling them about it, an easy, simple story for the world at large, as well as for them. As they had cleared away all the reasonable objections which I could bring forward, I was obliged to give them my word of honor that some day I would do so.

One of my best-founded objections was this, that some malicious persons would say, "Is there any real need of such a book?" To these my friends answered, "Even so! If others do not want it, we demand it of you,—write it just for us!"

And so I keep my word. I know full well

that others will not succeed exactly as I have, and I believe that it is not necessary for all children to be educàted just like my son. But I am convinced that much of what I have done may be repeated, and that an intelligent application of my method will be of no small use.

Pestalozzi became interested in me at a very early time, and with his clear vision and warm, unprejudiced mind naturally foresaw the plant, and even the fruit, while it still was in its tender bud, and so, while but very few paid any attention to what I was doing, expressed himself about it with great sympathy and even emphasis. Here are his words:

DEAR FRIEND:

Let me tell you once more, while you are still in our neighborhood, how much I am interested in the method of education which you are applying to your child, and how much I find our pedagogical ideas essentially the same. Let me say more than that: I have more than once been afraid that the rubric of my form, number and word, like the external form of my elementary books, at first sight seems to lead far away from the simple course of artless Nature and its best adherents, from the plain forms of common sense. However, this is certainly only an appearance, for in the execution our activity universally and most surely resembles every educational method in which the experiences of a father capable of strict observation and the heart of a truly loving mother find their pure expression. What of it, if this does not appear in the dead tables and heaping numerical series? It cannot appear there! But if Kruesi, guided by these forms, becomes all child to the child's mind, and the child finds himself in every word of Kruesi and, for the sake of his educational method, must find himself there, even as he must find himself in the simplest word of his mother, whose sense has become clear to him through a thousandfold experience,—then our real activity is indeed something quite different from what may seem from deceptive appearances. It is this, my friend, that you have seen better than any one else, even because you have been working essentially in the same spirit. You did not know it, but at the base of your activity lies the same matured natural feeling out of which, after endless seeking, my pedagogical forms have evolved.

My friend! Your work is very important. At this time we need more than anything else the proving of the work of education by matured experiences, and such experiences are calculated to rectify any views that are held in regard to my method. Under these circumstances you, my friend, must feel how important it is for me that you should continue the circle of your educational experiences and, if possible, should expand it. You have been invited to take up this career, independently from my wishes. Permit me, therefore, to add my wishes to those of your nearest friends, and urgently to ask you not to reject any opportunity that may offer itself to you. Much may be done by men like you, who with their astuteness grasp everything that presents itself to their minds, and who are able consistently to act in conformity with what they thus have abstracted, as agreeing both with the essence of human nature and the circumstances of human situations. I consciously count you among men of this sort, and at all events rejoice in advance at the chance of hearing from you about the progress of your experiences with the sincerity and definiteness that characterized you during the pleasant hours which I passed with you in discussing this subject.

May your journey across our mountains be happy, and may you be assured of the continuance of my sincere and lasting attachment.

Your loving friend,

PESTALOZZI.

August, 1804.

He has remained in this opinion for fourteen years, and has even lately urged me in private to make the story of my son's education as detailed and universal as possible. In this he was joined by his worthy friends and by the well-known French savant, Julien of Paris. They thoroughly met all my objections, which chiefly arose from timidity, and Pestalozzi wrote to me on the very day of my departure from Yverdon as follows:

MY DEAR MR. WITTE:

You, no doubt, remember the pedagogical conversation which we had fourteen years ago at Buchsee. You then gave us hope that, in accordance with your peculiar principles, you would carry your son's education much farther than is usual. Now the excellent progress made by him has far surpassed what you then dared to hope and utter.

The question arises, in how much has this progress been produced by your method of education, or been induced by it? The question arises, whether his progress is the direct result of his superior talent, and to what extent it is the result of pedagogical principles and means which, applied in the case of other children, would produce at least approximately similar results.

My dear Mr. Witte, you ought to put the friends of education in a position to judge with some degree of certainty, by giving them a detailed account, which would definitely enter into all the particulars, of how you have led your son from one step to another. There can be no doubt of your son's superior powers. But in how far your pedagogical skill seized these powers with psychological certainty and thus caused their rapid evolution, that can be made clear only by a very circumstantial story of what is peculiar and distinguishing in your method. It is important that this be done, and it is certainly the pleasantest business to which you may devote yourself.

Goodby, and may you be assured of the extreme consideration with which I have the honor to call myself

Your most humble servant and friend,

PESTALOZZI.

YVERDON, *September* 4, 1817

CHAPTER II

WAS MY SON BORN WITH EXTRAORDINARY APTITUDES?

I HAVE been told so an endless number of times, and should let it rest at that, for it is exceedingly pleasant to be able to say that one has been particularly favored by the Deity, or that one possesses a gift that enables him to do what nobody else can do. But to tell the truth this is not the case.

There are more than a thousand persons to whom I have denied it, and I must say that most of my friends and acquaintances were of this opinion. Only one man, Pastor Glaubitz, who had known me intimately in my childhood and who from 1788 to his death—that is, for a period of more than twenty years—had been a close friend of mine, used to say:

"I am convinced that Karl has no extraordinary aptitudes, and I am not one of those who marvel at his progress as at a miracle. On the contrary. I tell myself, you, and all who wish to hear it, that his aptitudes are only mediocre, but that his progress could not help being what it is, and the results of your education will in time appear even more brilliant. I know your educational plans and your way of doing things. They must succeed, unless God wants to hinder them."

Shortly before the birth of my son there were in the learned schools of Magdeburg (Kloster Liebenfrauen, Kloster Bergen and the Domschule) a number of young instructors of great ability. Other young men had lately taken positions as preachers in the neighborhood, and stood in friendly relations with these institutions. They all formed a fine circle which zealously occupied itself with man's most exalted business, that of his education. My friend Glaubitz had joined it, and through him I had been introduced to its meetings every time I could be there.

The conversation once turned upon this, that teachers and educators with their best wills at times could not accomplish anything, whereas, in my opinion, too much stress was put on man's natural aptitudes. In accordance with my observations, I was obliged to contradict them. I spoke as follows:

"The natural aptitudes have less to do with it than the child's education in his first five or six years. Of course, there is a difference in regard to the aptitudes, but, as a rule, that is, with such as most men are born with, infinitely more depends upon education than is usually believed."

To have a great authority on my side, I quoted, when pushed to it, the statement of Helvetius, "Chaque homme communément bien organisé peut devenir grand homme, suppose qu'il soit élevé comme il faut." Everybody was against me. When Mr. Schrader went home with Glaubitz and me, we still discussed the matter, and I repeated what I had said more than once in the meeting, where I was outvoted:

"Now I naturally must keep quiet, for there are thirteen or fourteen of you against me. But I hope to prove to you in fact that I am right. If God grants me a son, and if he, in your own opinion, is not to be called stupid,—which Heaven forfend,—I have long ago decided to educate him to be a superior man, without knowing in advance what his aptitudes may be."

They had taken me at my word in the meeting, and Schrader did the same now. Glaubitz had previously only indicated that he was not averse from my views. Now he attempted to convince Schrader that I would certainly keep my promise. But the latter, like all his friends, asserted that such a thing was impossible.

Shortly afterward Schrader learned from Glaubitz that a son had been born to my wife. He informed his friends of the fact, and they all watched me and my boy. Every time I came to their part of the country or Glaubitz came to see me, I was asked of the state of affairs, and heads wagged suspiciously whenever he or I gave hopes of fulfilling my old promise.

When Karl was four or five years old, I took him to Klein-Ottersleben. Mr. Schrader saw him and became very fond of him. Although he felt that the boy had no extraordinary aptitudes, he was sure that I should succeed in making much of him. Thus it went on until the year 1810. With every succeeding year Schrader convinced himself more and more that I was solving my problem, and in the latter year he so expressed himself in writing to me.

The letter is the more striking and remarkable since his personal observation and the information received from his and my intimate friends compelled him to admit that what I had promised and he had doubted had actually taken place, although he none the less could not make up his mind entirely to give up his prejudices and that of his friends. He remained to some extent my opponent. It, therefore, does his intellect and heart honor when he enthusiastically admits what has taken place, although he previously considered such a thing to be impossible. Here are his own words.

LANGENWEDDINGEN, *June* 3, 1810

HONORED FRIEND:

You have kept your word! Your Karl has become what you promised before his birth he would become, nay, he has done even better. When, ten years ago, you declared to me ecstatically in the presence of our deceased friend Glaubitz that you were hoping soon to be a father and that you fervently wished to be the father of a healthy son, you added the unforgettable words, "If my son will be healthily organized, I am determined to educate him to be a superior man."

I then contradicted you, saying that the success of your favorite plan did not depend alone on the health of the boy you were expecting, but more especially on his natural aptitudes. To this you replied: "Chaque homme communément bien organisé peut devenir grand homme, suppose qu'il soit élevé comme il faut." I continued to express my doubts, but Glaubitz assured me that you had already transformed a boy in Switzerland in a short time into a more than common man, although he had been given up by his former educators as almost stupid. I then promised you that I would delay my judgment until your boy should some day appear himself and speak for or against your assertion. Here he is, your boy. I see him in manly maturity, with childlike innocence and goodness in a rare union,—a charming picture of ennobled humanity! O lead me into a room filled with such men, and I shall deem myself to be removed from earth and in company of higher spirits!

Yes, my friend! You have not merely kept your word, you have accomplished more than you had promised. I feel myself under obligation to declare so in writing, in order to do you due justice. However, brilliant as the success of your endeavors has been, you will not be able to convince the pedagogues of the truth of your fundamental theory. They will say on all sides, "How happy is the father to whom such a son was born!" They will ascribe the boy's advantages more to the nature and aptitudes of the child, than to his father's art and deserts. And, to tell you frankly, I, too, am one of those who say: "If Karl had not been fortunately organized, he would not have become that which he now is." I know your by no means small deserts in regard to him. I know your power, your rare patience, the firm persistency with which you pursue your purpose. I know that this boy was the point around which all your previous life with all its activity has gyrated; that you have known how to bring everything, speech and silence, coming and going, work and rest, everything that surrounds the boy, into nearer or more remote relations to him and to your purpose; that you have for years labored untiringly, uninterruptedly, with ever-constant powers and vivacity. Besides, I know the mighty power which you exert with your exceptional persistency on all those on whom you wish to exert it,—and yet, in spite of all that, I cannot disagree with those pedagogues.

It is not only difficult, but, indeed, entirely impossible to determine the relative part played by Nature and art in the education of man, because during the process of education they stand in interrelation with each other. You will forever want proof by which to make it clear that you have educated a healthy, but not favorably or fortunately organized, boy by means of the art of treatment alone to become a superior man. None the less your experiment will in every respect remain remarkable and important for pedagogy, and a detailed account of your method will be a valuable gift to the public. Naturally it will take a Witte to carry this method into execution, and so I warrant you that you will have few imitators.

SCHRADER,

Preacher at Langenweddingen near Magdeburg.

CHAPTER III

DID MY EDUCATIONAL WORK PROCEED SUCCESSFULLY?

THE way I instructed and educated my son must not only have had a good beginning, but must also have proceeded successfully, since the attention of the cultured, and even the active participation of different, nay, mutually hostile, governments have now for more than ten years been bestowed upon me.

When my son first became talked about, in his eighth year, we were living in a village, Lochau, near Halle, in surroundings which certainly were not calculated in themselves to direct the attention of the public upon a child. Such a thing may take place more easily in a city, especially a large city.

Besides, Karl's unusual education fell into a period when Europe was shaken in its very foundation, and when our country, Prussia, was almost crushed. I am speaking of the years 1807 and 1808. People had then other subjects for entertainment. Great, terrible occurrences, anxieties, hopes, longings for help, disappointments,—only such things appeared remarkable. Trifles were overlooked.

The attainments of a child must have been very considerable, they must have been extraordinary, if they were to pass through these epochal events, find a place for themselves, and become established. And this they have done.

That point of time was particularly unfavorable, for there was then a distinct prejudice against early maturity of learning. Men like Salzmann, Campe, Trapp, had for a long time spoken against it with emphasis and had objectively pointed out the uselessness and harm of earlier examples, and had stigmatized them as products of "hot-house education."

As I myself considered it an honor to have been their disciple, I am willing to admit that I shared their opinion in this very matter, and that I had my misgivings when I saw something taking place under my guidance of which I was afraid.

Consequently the first news of it in the public papers (the letter of an unknown person in the *Hamburger Correspondent* giving an exact account of my son's public and private examination in Merseburg) was considered untrue and senseless. A Danish savant even denied the whole fact and believed that he must deny it from inner causes. That which seemed incredible, however, soon gained credence, when repeated examinations drew forth the many testimonials, personally signed by such men as Schuetz, Tieftrunk, Cæsar, Bek, Mahlmann, Rost, and a mass of excellent men, to which learned societies and universities were soon added. Soon voices rose on all sides for the good cause, and it was accepted as an established fact.

The particular period was also most unfavorable, because the war and its sad consequences had unsettled everything. Prussia seemed forever destroyed. Its inhabitants were daily drained more and more, and I was living at the extreme end of the monarchy, for Lochau was on all sides surrounded by Saxony. There could be no thought of support, and yet I had to leave the village, if Karl was not to stagnate, that is, to go back.

I could not count on Prussia. France wanted to get money, not to give it, while Saxony could hardly have the wish to do something, since I in no way stood in physical need. I had a good parish and the written assurance of a still better one to come. I lived quite comfortably and enjoyed with my family,—even in Leipsic,—all the pleasures of my station of life.

Meanwhile my son's education was still in its germ. Countless people feared evil consequences. "In his tenth or twelfth year the poor child will die or waste away!" they frequently said, in a truly anxious manner.

Nevertheless, the city and the university of Leipsic united in a very surprising way, and by a considerable stipend for my son and very kind and advantageous offers for me and my wife made it possible for me to give up my parish and to make up my mind to go to live in Leipsic. Every sensible person will surmise that this was not done without most careful investigations and repeated tests of my son.

The French Westphalian government proceeded in the same manner. It examined my son repeatedly and with suspicion, but ended by offering me monetary support, which was regularly paid out to me, even on the day when the Russians were firing on Kassel.

When Westphalia collapsed, my patrons and friends took care of me and my son, for Prussia, my fatherland, which for seven years had methodically been sucked dry and exhausted, was in the midst of a doubtful war, while Hanover, Brunswick, and Hesse hastened to make it known that every stranger from another state should repair home, and violently rejected any demands made upon them on the basis of Westphalian recommendations. Yet all three states promptly and freely paid to me what I asked of them on the basis of those recommendations, after having, most naturally and reasonably, first convinced themselves that the money, of which they were very much in need, was well spent in my case.

Then many Prussians of the upper class encouraged me to turn to our monarch. The times being so unpropitious, I did not dare do so for a long while. Finally, having been urged anew, I made a cautious inquiry, and I received a most magnanimous and encouraging answer. Indeed, after a closer investigation of the matter, I was granted more than I had dared to ask. How gracious the proofs of royal attention and favor have been, which my son and I have for the last two years enjoyed here in Berlin!

Since all this has been maintained without interruption for the period of ten years, since the most different, and mutually opposed men, savants and statesmen, even monarchs, have united for prompt and active coöperation, the cause for which such sacrifices have sympathetically been made must be good and must have succeeded.

A mass of written congratulations and expressions of heartfelt interest, which came chiefly from men whom I did not personally know, a mass of personal proofs of kindness, well-wishing, respect, and sincere sympathy, attest the fact that my undertaking was continuously successful. It has won for itself the noble ones of our own land and other countries, or my eyes, ears, senses, and intellect must have egregiously deceived me.

CHAPTER IV

Is my Son's Education Finished?

So far as I am concerned, it is. I have long withstood those who asserted that it was finished, but now I must admit it is. When he was eleven years old, several professors at Goettingen thought that it was not necessary for me any longer to accompany my son to his lectures, that he behaved perfectly well, was attentive, made the proper notes, and I, therefore, could spare myself the trouble. None the less I used to go with him, made all the preparations for the lectures and all the reviews together with him. Later, at Goettingen and at Heidelberg, I stopped it all, but I proceeded very slowly and imperceptibly, before leaving him entirely to his own actions.

Only after he had made his appearance several times as an author in difficult matters, evoking respect and applause, only after he had received honors, such as are usually bestowed upon a real savant of advanced years, only after Our Majesty, the King, and his minister considered him worthy to undertake a two-years' scientific journey at the expense of the state, and that he, then sixteen years old, was fully able to take care of himself,— did I make up my mind to consider his education finished so far as I was concerned, and resolved at last seriously to consider my own health.

However, not to be too rash and do things prematurely, of which I had constantly been in fear, I wrote to our honored monarch that from considerations which I adduced I should like to keep my son another year with me, in order that he might have an opportunity to prepare himself as thoroughly for this distinguished mission as he had formerly prepared himself for every important change in his intellectual life. His Majesty gave the necessary consent with a readiness and liberality which throw a bright light both on the correct view and on the noble heart of the monarch. It was only then that, with the approval of my patrons and friends, I left the house and city in which my son was living.

I have been away from him for seventeen

months, and during that time I saw him only once in Vienna on his journey to Switzerland and Italy.

Not to push him out into the world all at once, while he was still so young, and in order not to make the change from the considerate care of both parents to the absolute self-dependence among strangers too sudden, I left him during my absence with his mother and in the circle of noble friends, who fortunately belonged to all classes of society and to all ages, and recommended to him that in the proper season he should at my expense take trips to Leipsic and Dresden and to their charming surroundings, Freiburg, Chemnitz, Naumburg, Jena, Weimar, Erfurth, Gotha, Liebenstein, Eisenach, Kassel, Goettingen, Brunswick, Magdeburg, Salzwedel, etc., should inspect all kinds of works of nature and of art, and should make use of libraries and gain personal acquaintance with scholars, —in short, should practically prepare himself for his great journey, and then should in four or five months return to his mother in Berlin, in order once more to begin and continue the theoretical preparation. All that he did advantageously to himself, and in May of this year he actually started on his greater journey. After having been with him in Vienna for two months, I forever told him goodby, and he is now living beyond the Alps. I obviously can no longer supervise him. He stands alone, in the care of God and his own conscience. I must, therefore, assume that his education is completed, in so far as I am concerned.

Of course, that education which we all receive until our death, that perfection which we obtain through the circumstances of life, our vicissitudes, our acquaintances, our converse with the living and the dead,—that education has naturally not been finished and cannot be finished.

When I started on my journey of seventeen months, he was bodily and spiritually in perfect health, sound and joyful, and worked with pleasure and ease. He had never been ill, and had not even had the diseases of infancy.

CHAPTER V

Every Ordinarily Organized Child may Become a Superior Man, if He is Properly Educated

THIS is a proposition which I maintained before a large company of educators at Magdeburg, before my son was born, and which I have since repeatedly defended. To speak with Helvetius, "Every ordinarily organized child may become a superior man, if only he is excellently educated."

I know very well that the keys of a piano that have no strings cannot respond, no matter how skilful the player may be. I just as certainly know that an expert can easily remedy a great dissonance and elicit an agreeable melody from an instrument that before sounded wretchedly. The particular instrument may not have that perfect structure that distinguishes some other instrument, but if the first is properly tuned, while the second becomes more out of order every moment, a piece of music played on the first will be more agreeable to the ear than one played on the other.

To speak without similes. If a child's body or mind lacks an organ, it will be impossible even for the greatest educator on earth to bring out that which it is the property of that organ to develop. But if all the organs are present, some of them, however, in a weaker degree and without the proper perfection, and in their active power, be it of a corporal or spiritual nature, are somewhat behind the others,—the clear-sighted educator, but only such, may be able by degrees completely to overcome these deficiencies, or, at least, to produce results which would startle the man of reason who has known the organ in its former state and now becomes aware of the greatly improved results.

Such an educator will be able to raise a child of mediocre organization by means of a very careful treatment to a degree of education which excellently organized children, under a careless and improper method of education, frequently do not attain. Hence it must, as a rule, turn out to be true that a child of mediocre organization who has been educated with much love, cleverness, attention, and zeal by a very skillful and cautious educator may, in the realm of beings, finally occupy a higher position than a highly organized child who has been carelessly and badly educated by thoughtless and inexperienced educators. On the other hand, it must be self-evident that the latter could and must have risen much higher if it had been treated as wisely and as carefully as the first. And it is equally clear that this too frequently fails to happen in our imperfect world, that, indeed, it cannot happen under the existing circumstances. It is therefore obvious that many well organized children go backward, and become unreasoning, ignorant, and even bad, while some ordinarily organized children through favorable circumstances rise to a point reached but by few mortals.

What a most fortunately organized man may become under the most appropriate education and most favorable circumstances, that, I assert, we do not know at all, for our Alexanders, Cæsars, Charlemagnes, Henrys, Fredericks, had their weak, or, more correctly, their bad sides. Consequently they came very much short of that ideal which is possible even in our imperfect world. I am convinced that an exceptionally well-educated man would be greater, stronger, healthier, more beautiful, gentler, more courageous, more magnanimous, nobler, braver, wiser, wittier, more earnest, more learned, sensible, moderate, restrained (of course, everything in its right place),—in short, that he would be a man who would stand incomparably nearer to the higher beings than we do.

If we were a hundred years advanced in the art of education, my proposition would, perhaps, be wrong. Perhaps it would not be, for it would still be a question whether all the means for awakening and educating all the powers that are latent in every child had been found and had become a common property, and whether there were many parents and educators who had conscientiously used every opportunity for the advancement of those under their charge from their cradle to their completed education. Only then would it be possible to assert that a father of an ordinarily organized child could not accomplish anything more for him than ten other fathers of very favorably organized children did for their own, and so could not advance his son any farther, and had, on the contrary, to let him fall behind the others.

But this is not the case now. We are still very far from being able to assert that others could not accomplish still more. There will hardly be a sensible, especially an experienced, man who will not, in applying a system of education, discover that he has committed some blunders which have been injurious to his pupil and have visibly kept him from becoming what he otherwise might have turned out to be.

If, now, it is quite certain that our usual method of education and instruction is still far behind that which an individual man may accomplish, because he exerts all his powers in the desire to obtain results,—then it is quite comprehensible that such a man would be able to promote the lesser aptitudes better than the greater aptitudes are generally promoted at present: that he, therefore, may be able to educate a child with ordinary organization so as to become a superior man.

But since my proposition, of which I am as convinced as of my existence, has been universally attacked, although a very few persons, without my aid, have grasped it correctly and put it in the clearest light, I am constrained to believe that people have generally misunderstood it, albeit claiming to understand it, and, as usual, have brought forward a mass of objections which frequently destroy one another and frequently are so weak that upon closer examination they collapse as untenable.

So I will try to explain it at greater length, by reproducing as faithfully as possible one of the many conversations I have in the last twenty-five years had upon the subject.

Mr. A. "No, my friend, you cannot convince me of it. For from this it would follow that all men are born with equal aptitudes,—and who could assume such a thing? The diversity of human aptitudes is self-evident."

I. "To me also. But you are mistaken in assuming that your conclusion actually followed from my proposition."

He. "What? You mean to say that my conclusion is wrong? Is it not clear that all children must have equal aptitudes, if I can educate every one of them to be a superior man?"

I. "In the first place, I did not say that

you could do so with every child, for I know that there are cretins, who we also call human beings; I know very well that the gradation from these to the man who comes into the world with the highest possible perfection of organization is enormous; I know that we are unable to count all the rounds of such a ladder."

He. "You mean to say that this was not your idea? Then I must have misunderstood you very much."

I. "That you have, for I keep saying 'from every healthily organized child,' and that makes a great difference."

He. "I do not find it so, or I do not understand you."

I. "The latter may easily be the case. So I will try to make myself clearer. I assume with you that men's aptitudes are very different, that, if we consider all their bodily, mental, and moral aptitudes singly and in their interactions, we truly may say that their diversities cannot be counted. But for our purposes we must consider them capable of mensuration. Let us, therefore, assume a diversity grading from one to one hundred. The above-mentioned cretin may be considered as having an aptitude of one, while the best-organized man possesses one of one hundred. Then an ordinarily organized child may be regarded as having an aptitude of——"

He. "Fifty. That is clear. But of what good is that?"

I. "You will soon hear. So I assume that many children come into the world with aptitudes graded as fifty, for what is most ordinary is most frequent. Thus your son, mine, and the son of uncountable others would belong to this number."

He. "Not at all. I will admit this in the case of my son, but not of yours."

I. "Very well. To please you, I will for the present say nothing about it. But, let us proceed! Think of ten or a dozen children whose aptitudes are fifty, but in various relations. Let two of them be brought up in the country, entirely without any instruction; two others, with not much more instruction, in the city, employed from earliest childhood as apprentices in a factory; two of them educated in a poor school, two in a better school; two others, carefully and well brought up in the family circle; finally, two who have been wrongly educated at home. You will easily perceive that, if the aptitudes are everything and education can do but little or nothing at all, all these ten or twelve children should at the end of their education be at the same level, while one of these may become prince or minister, another a scholar, a third a merchant, a ninth a beggar, and a tenth a robber. But do you believe that all ten would be standing on the same level of human perfection?"

He. "Naturally not. For one will have learned much, another—little, a third—nothing at all; hence one will become an excellent man, another—an ordinary, a third—a bad man."

I. "So you observe from this example how much education may do. But let us overlook this too. Will their natural aptitudes, which originally were absolutely the same, still be absolutely the same after the course of twenty years?"

He. "What do you mean?"

I. "I mean, for example, will all ten boys at their twentieth year be possessed of the same corporal strength?"

He. "How could this be possible? We are speaking only of what is ordinary, of the natural, as they call it. Obviously the son of the robber, the day-laborer, and the peasant will, as a rule, have surprisingly greater bodily strength than the son of the artist, the scholar, and the minister."

I. "Very well! But why?"

He. "That is clear. Because the first three have naturally been developing their bodily strength, and in their particular situations could not help developing it. In the case of the other three, the bodily strength will, no doubt, be exercised but little or not at all, hence it will remain latent or die out completely."

I. "So you admit that power, say, bodily power, will increase in proportion as it is put to use."

He. "Certainly! It is the same as in the case of the magnet. The more a magnet is given by degrees to attract—of course, within the extreme limits of what a magnet can bear—the more it will attract."

I. "Well, this is a great gain for me, for you admit that the inborn powers of man, that is, his aptitudes, develop only in proportion as they are put into activity and brought out by his educators."

He. "Who could deny this? But how is this against me?"

I. "It is not against you, but it helps me very much in the establishment of my proposition, for it follows from it that all that is necessary is in the most careful and even manner, from the cradle on, to develop a child's natural aptitudes, in order to educate a man who will stand much higher than all the others who are endowed with the same natural aptitudes."

He. "You are mistaken. The case is merely possible, but no conclusion can be drawn from what is possible to what actually is."

I. "I beg your pardon. You are mistaken, for we are not yet speaking of the reality. You have already admitted the possibility, and this is all I want."

He. "My friend, you seem to entangle me with invisible threads, and then you will all of a sudden cry out, 'Caught!' But that will not do! If your assertion contains an inner truth, you must proceed openly with me."

I. "I have done so all along, and I intend to proceed in the same manner. Here is the proof of it. We started with your denial of the proposition that it was possible to make a superior man out of any healthily organized child, provided he is properly educated."

He. "Right, and I still deny it!"

I. "So we have come to an agreement that men come into the world with the most diverse aptitudes of body, mind, and heart; that the very favorably as well as the very unfavorably organized children form the minority, while the ordinarily organized form the majority. We have assumed a scale of aptitudes from one to one hundred, placing those of the cretin at one, the most favorably endowed human nature at birth at one hundred, and the endowment of most children at fifty; and you have granted to me that among ten children of the latter kind there will soon appear an enormous diversity of the growth of their powers, in proportion as this or that has received particular attention; that some powers would completely stagnate, if they were not used or developed, or were even repressed. Is this so?"

He. "Yes, yes! But what follows from it?"

I. "What I have deduced from it, namely, that all that is necessary is evenly and with great care to educate the natural powers of a child, that is, his aptitudes, in order to make a superior man of him."

He "Very well! I admit that such a child will in time stand higher than those who began with the same aptitudes, but who were later badly educated. But what does this prove against me? I may assume that among these ten boys five are educated very well. And you will certainly not deny that such a case is possible?"

I. "I might deny it, for it is a rare thing for one to be educated very well. However, I will grant you this, in the ordinary sense of the word. But I cannot do so in the sense in which I take it, for I understand under an especially good education one in which already the child's father has, either by fate or by his parents, been educated uncommonly well; in which he possesses the needed health, time, knowledge, and experience to be able to give an exceptionally good education; in which he, besides, brings an inner inclination and an iron will for the education of his child; and in which he appropriately chooses his vocation, his domicile, his consort, his chief and secondary occupations, his friends, his acquaintances, and even his servants. He must be able and willing to live, now as a hermit, now in traveling, now in the great world, now in the country, now in a provincial town, now at the university, now in the capital. Only then can there be an education such as I have in mind, an entirely exceptional one, by means of which all the child's powers may be developed in the widest and most even manner.

"It was my ideal to be able to change at any moment, in conformity with the circumstances, and I am grateful to Providence that I was granted the chance at least to approach my goal. But I should gladly have given my son an education in which I should have been able to make these changes with infinitely greater rapidity, every time they appeared necessary to me. But you will easily understand that that far exceeded my powers, that is, my ability; and it is only under such conditions that it would have been possible for me to develop all his aptitudes evenly, to the utmost limits of their perfectibility."

He. "Very well! But who can do so?"

I. "It is not impossible, as you will admit. But if a child were educated in this manner, it would become evident that education placed him above all those with whom he once was equal."

He. "Yes, if I should assume that there exists such a wise, learned, able, good-hearted, and iron-willed father, you would be right; his education would place his child above all those who formerly were equal with him. But you have gained little by this, for your proposition says a great deal more. According to it a child thus educated would also have to surpass those who are born with the aptitudes rated at sixty, seventy, eighty, and ninety. You see, I am magnanimous enough to rate your son at one hundred.

I. "Do not do that! I shall accept what you have to say in so far as it is true. We shall soon see in how far you are right. I said: 'Every ordinarily organized child may become a superior man, if he is educated exceptionally well.' A superior man does not mean the first, second, or third man in the whole kingdom. One may be satisfied if he towers over thousands, which he certainly will, for the children who are born with aptitudes of eighty, eighty-five, ninety, ninety-five, and one hundred are certainly as rare as those, thank Heaven, who are by Nature stepmotherly endowed with aptitudes of twenty-five, twenty, fifteen, ten, five, and one. Consider more especially that many children are born and live with excellent aptitudes under such circumstances as make their aptitudes not only useless, but even harmful to them."

He. "How so?"

I. "The superior mental power will more easily harm than help the son of the robber, beggar, and poor day laborer. It can hardly be properly developed, on account of the unfortunate circumstances under which they live. Consequently it will look for a side path, just as a seed does when it has a stone weighing upon it. And this side path is only too often a bad one. The more mental aptitudes such a man possesses, the more I tremble for him, for what under other circumstances ennobles the land and supports the throne, will easily deteriorate into trickiness, wiles, and rascality. This will happen the more certainly, the more powerfully and the quicker his mind asserts itself, for the necessary props of religion, of internal and external morality are lacking in him. He has not been accustomed to voluntary renunciation, acquiescence in submission to God, or wise patience. The stronger he is, the more certainly he will try to crush his surroundings, and what might have ended in laurels and stars will lead him to the branding, the gallows, and the rack. Hence all the favorably organized children who are born under such and similar circumstances are not to be considered at all, for they will not outshine the best-educated man with aptitudes of fifty.

"Let us now ascend to the higher strata of society. The extremes generally meet. It is true that the children of the upper classes could be educated by far in the best manner, but are they? I wish I were obliged to answer, Yes. Of course, in their case there are very many means for doing so. I am speaking of the external means, wealth, opportunity to see and hear many interesting things, to converse with superior men, and to make use of everything which advances the mind. If the parents also possessed the internal means, and if these were honestly applied, the children of these upper classes would of necessity become the best. If, therefore, there is a distinguished and wealthy father who does not want or is unable himself to give his son a good education, and is wise enough to choose a superior educator from the middle class, who will be a father to his son in the best sense of the word, and if he is fortunate enough to find such a one, then let him spend on him what he can spend on himself,—he will not pay too much for him. I assume, above all else, that he gives this educator a free hand and that the educator does his duty. If the boy's aptitudes are excellent, so much the better. If they are mediocre, such an educator is so much the more needed. If they are slight, he is indispensable. But how often have I seen such means neglected!

"In the choice of an educator they do not always ask, Which is the better? but frequently, Which is the cheaper? Which one has the most suave manners? or even, From what country does he come, or to what caste does he belong? Other parents circumscribe his free activity in regard to his charge. Others forget the respect and friendship which they owe him, and in all these cases hurt the child without retrieve.

"And where is the upper-class family which would have the will and strength,—I will not say! on account of their son to sacrifice their own connections, prejudices, comforts, distractions, and the sensuous enjoyments, which present themselves every day in another form to them,—but only firmly to remove these from their son? Are not most children of this type satiated before they have become youths? And if the parents have given them the inheritance of pure blood, is it not too often polluted in their earliest years, and are not their bodies so weakened that they turn out to be feeble, pale house-dolls whom the first northerner throws to the ground, although with such educational means there should have resulted young Hercules with the mental powers of an Apollo?

"We do not meet with many youths of the latter kind in upper-class society, and yet they should be common there; they should the more splendidly increase in mind as in years, because the opportunity to hear, see, and experience, hence to train and exercise the mind, presents itself to them every day; and because they are placed in offices which should be of help to them, since the activities associated with these ought to sharpen their intellect, increase their insight, and make them capable of acting and participating in great things.

"With a little bit of reflection you will find, my friend, that I should have to fear much from this side, but in reality there is nothing to fear. In the upper classes of society there are really not many youths, perhaps not even children, who betray superior powers in body, mind and heart. Or are you of a different opinion?"

He. "Unfortunately not. But what has that to do with our matter?"

I. "It proves to you that if a child with an aptitude of fifty is really brought up as well as a child might be, he some day will tower above the youth of the upper classes, even if they were born with aptitudes of eighty, ninety, and one hundred."

He. "Very, very bad it is, but I cannot find you wrong in it."

I. "Thus we have left only the children of the well-to-do middle class. Since this class is the pith of the nation, I must dwell here a little longer. Children from the well-to-do middle class may reach a high degree of development. But here there takes place what I mentioned before: I should be wrong if the art of education had already advanced so far that parents or educators usually accomplished everything which man is capable of accomplishing. This is so far from being the case that I may truly say that untold times they fail completely. I frequently marvel how it is possible for intelligent parents to act so wrongly, and yet this is a daily occurrence. I tell them so, and they do not listen to me, or they listen and feel it, but do not act accordingly.

"As long as the parents love one child more than another; as long as their love is more sensuous than intelligent, more animal than human; as long as their money, or their honors in the state, or their pleasures and their society are more to them than their children;—so long will they never succeed in developing to the highest degree all the powers of their children alike, and so long will the one who is less endowed by nature, if everything has been done for him that can be done, of a surety rise above the others, even if their natural aptitudes surpass his own.

"Add to this that a vivacious mind fails

more easily than an inert one, and that it will more easily transgress and will issue from its transgressions with greater difficulty,—and you will at once see that a man who has been educated according to the ideal which the perfect educator has in mind will not so easily find another one who surpasses him."

He. "Certainly. But you must admit that another person with greater aptitudes would advance much farther if he enjoyed the same good education."

I. "No doubt about that!"

He. "Well, how far would he advance?"

I. "To a degree of perfection which is still unknown to us. What causes us to make complex calculations, such a man would see through in a moment; what to us is hard work, would be to him easy, pleasant play. Nothing but the limitations of human nature would keep him in bounds."

He. "Do you believe that a man could be educated so far?"

I. "Why should I not? I should have to deny a wise and kind God, if I did not believe it. I not only believe it, but I am absolutely convinced of it."

He. "Well, I do not believe it, because it would be productive of much unhappiness."

I. "Unhappiness? What unhappiness?"

He. "Much, very much unhappiness! Both in the upper and in the lower classes of society."

I. "You make me very curious, because I do not see it."

He. "I am surprised, for it seems so clear."

I. "So I beg you earnestly to inform me of it."

He. "Gladly. You assume that there could be men who would be like angels, who everywhere recognize the truth without prejudice; who everywhere ask only what is right, true, beautiful, good, sensible, proper, in accordance with duty, and so forth, and who, finally, consider as play and do far better what to us is hard work. You consider this possible, do you not?"

I. "Very possible. Indeed, I hope that in a hundred years there will be many such men, if universal instruction and especially education continue to advance in the right direction."

He. "Then I pity poor humanity, for we shall have to pass through another revolution."

I. "Why so?"

He. "Very naturally so. There will arise men,—I follow out your ideas,—who will stand infinitely higher than all their fellows——"

I. "I must interrupt you. Not so very much higher! Not more than at present our men of superior education surpass the others. You must not forget that I have added the condition, If universal instruction and especially education continue to advance in the right direction. If such is the case, the whole will remain in equipoise. The man of superior education will, of course, stand higher than the man of superior education at present; but the whole human race of his time will also stand higher, hence will come as close to him as the present race approaches the most cultured man of our time."

He. "This somewhat softens my objection, but it does not remove it. In any case such a man will stand startlingly higher, hence he will want to drag humanity up to him. In other words, he will wish to introduce universally justice, truth, beauty, goodness, reason, equity, duty, and if he is opposed he will call forth a revolution or will be taken to the insane asylum."

I. "Either will be likely only in the same degree in which it is at present and has been ever since the world has existed. Extraordinary men have shaken the moral world more than once. But as long as we believe in a Providence, we must assume that it permitted this to happen for the best of humanity. Besides, do not forget that I said that all the powers of a man educated in a superior way must be developed evenly. If this is done, his heart will certainly not be poor in goodness, meekness, and patience, and in such a case love and sympathy for his fellowmen will soften the rough edges and sharp points in his desires and acts."

He. "But if this should not happen?"

I. "Since you proceed from our supposition that in a superior system of education all the powers are symmetrically developed, your objection does not touch me. But I may allow it to be valid, and yet it does not embarrass me."

He. "Indeed?"

I. "Yes. You will admit that a sharp knife may be used as much for good as for evil, for eating as for killing, will you not? Am I to honor and respect less the artist who has made it, on account of its possible misuse?"

He. "Certainly not."

I. "My son was permitted to drink wine during long walks and before, during, and after exhaustive exertions. I almost encouraged him to do so, although he did not customarily drink wine. Let us assume the unfortunate case that he would become a drunkard, thus weakening in body and mind. Should I be blamed for having given him wine as medicine?"

He. "Not at all!"

I. "The art of writing, the invention of printing, powder, the discovery of America, and so forth, are all discoveries which, with the good which they have produced, have also caused much evil. Are they, on that account, to be hated or despised?"

He. "No, no!"

I. "Shall we, perhaps, do the way our fathers and mothers did thirty and forty years ago, when they purposely did not allow their daughters to learn writing, so that they would not be able to write love letters, and thus drove them into the nets of low cheats, lovelaces, and pimps?"

He. "Heaven forbid!"

I. "Well, then let us do what is good honestly and with all our power, trusting in God who will prevent the evil consequences or will lead to magnificent results. Shall we wish for no Washingtons and Franklins because they accomplished the revolution which has raised North America so highly on the throne of ennobled humanity, and will continue to raise it still more highly? 'If England, the ruler, had met her subject daughter halfway in a friendly manner, there would have been no revolution, and the happiness intended by the Deity would none the less have been attained.' In these words lies everything that I need to say, nay, even more than you think."

He. "Oh, I understand you, and you are perfectly right. The Heavens grant that this experience and other experiences like it may produce the result which they could and should produce!"

I. "I hope so, for humanity advances incessantly, and, thank Heaven, toward what is better. I can think only forty years back, but in these very forty years, as you know, a history of at least four hundred years has passed by us. I have lived to see mighty upheavals; I have more than once suffered terribly from them; and yet I aver that the present time is far preferable to that of old. As a man advanced in years I could easily foster prejudices for olden days; as an experienced man I know the thousandfold evils that have walked the earth,—and yet I bless that fate that has allowed me to live until now, for truth and reason have mightily fought their way forward. The rights of humanity are recognized, even where it is done with anger. The classes that once were treated by the laws as herds and were arbitrarily crushed, now stand up like men, for society has demanded and obtained consideration for them."

He. "True! Good and true! But this very turn of our conversation reminds me of another objection. Let us see whether you are able to remove this also!"

I. "Gladly! Only let me ask you first,

through whom have those splendid results, which you yourself recognize as such, been produced, through better or through worse men?"

He. "What do you mean by that?"

I. "What I mean to say by it does not belong here as yet. First of all we are concerned with what I say. So I ask you again, are these recognized excellent effects the work of men who were educated especially well or ill? Mind you, I include in education everything which time, place, circumstances, intercourse, incidents, and vicissitudes have done, thus aiding in the education.

He. "Now I understand you. Well, yes, through the most cultured, for I am not so foolish as to adduce the inhuman beings of the French atrocities against you."

I. "That you could not do, if you wanted to keep your eye on truth, justice, and equity. It was the superciliousness, stubbornness, and weakness of the opposite party which produced and fostered these abominations. As soon as they came into power, they first struck at the wiser and better men, because these always opposed their cruelty and unreason. Do not forget that wherever there is talk about a dragon, there is also mention made of a swamp and cave as producer and habitat of such a creature. Destroy the two from the start, and there will be no evil dragon! Destroy them later, and he will soon disappear, and the evils which he has been doing, because they did not proceed, rationally, will now at least be destroyed."

He. "I understand, and you are right. But now comes my objection. I wish you could overcome it, for it seems to me to be more important than the first."

I. "You would not have said so, perhaps, fifteen minutes ago. But let me hear it!"

He. "You assert that a time could and would come when individuals would in their development rise almost as high as the higher beings, that even the whole human race, at least whole nations, would attain a much higher degree of culture."

I. "Certainly! I hope for it as a man. I believe it as a man of experience. I am convinced of it, because I am a rational being, and believe in an almighty, all-wise, and all-good God."

He. "Very well! I do not deny it, it is

a beautiful, elevating idea. But where shall we then get our worker-bees from? For the worker-bees of the present—the lower strata of the people—will rise so highly in education that they will not be willing to work."

I. "You are mistaken, my friend! This can never happen in an all-sided education, and the one-sided one, which now is generally called enlightenment, is not to be considered by us, for, as I said, all the aptitudes of man are to be developed symmetrically, consequently the aptitudes of his heart, his disposition, his good will, his moral, his religious sense are to be equally developed, and as highly as possible. Virtue and fear of God, as well as love for men, for one's duties and for God must attain the highest perfection in one educated in a superior way. Consequently he will respect his calling, will love his duties, and will gladly perform the work of his vocation, in order to please the Highmost."

He. "My dear friend! I do not believe you in this. What? You mean to say that a very cultured man will be willing to dig, plow, harrow, mow, thresh, and so forth? Never!"

I. "You are mistaken. There have been shepherds who, with their most meager income, performed their still more lowly work faithfully and honestly, indeed, with sincere love for it, although they stood in real culture higher than many a general, minister, or prince."

He. "I should like to know of such a shepherd."

I. "You may easily know one. Read about David Klaus, the cowherd at Halberstadt, whose life has been described by Konsistorialrath Streithorst.

"A peasant of this kind was Kleinjogg, and I have known similar day laborers and workmen who rose far above their station of life and yet loved it sincerely and carried out their duties joyfully. And it has to be so if the education is of the right kind. A school-teacher and country preacher are certainly abused men, if they want to do their duties. They have a mass of trifling, mechanical labors to perform, hence a mass of very unpleasant affairs to deal with. The country preacher has even such duties to perform as endanger his health and his life. I have known men in both callings who, with the education of a Konsistorialrath and Professor, were obliged to struggle with want, and yet joyfully did everything for God's sake, do you understand me, my friend? for the sake of God who rules in their breasts as in the universe at large, in order to cultivate in the best manner possible this small corner in the great garden of the Deity, mindful of the promise, 'Thou hast been faithful in a very little, have thou authority over ten cities.'

"There is, therefore, no danger in true culture. The worker-bees will, as before, find a pleasant occupation in flying about in God's free air, in finding the flowers useful to them, and in industriously collecting the honey-juice and the wax-dust. They will find their pleasure and pride, as before, in accomplishing most for themselves and for the common weal. If this does not happen, the fault lies with our enlighteners.

"Suppose even that among them there will be some who will rise to an upper class, who will pass from the shepherd's staff to the pen, from the plow to the painter's brush or etcher's tool, what of it?"

He. "That is just what I have been waiting for. I say that it does do harm, for we shall soon have no manual workmen. There will be a lack of work-hands to produce and prepare the necessaries of life for us. We shall, therefore, go hungry, thirsty, and cold, because the lower classes have become too well educated, too refined, too tender, and too much ennobled, to be willing to stick to the clod of earth and dig in it."

I. "Rest calm, my friend! There will always be many who will want to remain worker-bees. I am assured of this by the diversity of natural aptitudes which will persist to the end of the world, and by the frailty of the human race, its inborn inclination toward indolence, its tendency to do that which is easiest, and our universal love for moving actively in the open. Hunting and fishing, no matter how low they stand in the scale of labor, are carried on with pleasure and with true passion, even by the highest men on earth. Nor have I any fear for wood-chopping, digging,—two sensible occupations of many learned men, in order to save themselves from hypochondria,—plowing, mowing, and threshing. There will always be found men who will like to do it. I am rather afraid that, with the higher perfection, we shall have too many unemployed hands."

He. "How curious you are! I should think that this did not follow from what you said before."

I. "Not directly, but certainly indirectly. We all know that there are countries even now where there are too many unemployed hands, because the higher culture pressed the fire, water, and air into service."

He. "Oh, you mean England."

I. "Yes, and a hundred other places as well. It was only yesterday that I visited a factory where one little steam engine was performing the work of three or four hundred persons, and was performing it better than they possibly could. But they have already built a second one in the same factory, which will throw out more than one thousand persons. Who knows but that in one hundred and fifty years we shall be able to dig, harrow, plow, mow, bind, transport, and so forth, by means of machinery, even as it is now the case with propelling and paving."

He. "You put the weapons into my hand, for I rightly ask you: How are we going to occupy the superfluous hands? There will be many of them, for there are here and there even now more than needed, and human culture will still continue to grow, and the human race is said to be on an annual increase. Thus, for example, inoculation against small-pox now saves the lives of hundreds who would otherwise have died."

I. "My dear friend, this is God's business. If He has given us the power and the will to rise higher, it is our duty to do so. It is His business to see to it that the whole does not lose its balance. And He will certainly do so. A hundred years ago people would have considered it impossible to be happy under the circumstances which we have lived through, hence we need not worry uselessly over what may happen in another hundred years. But we should be acting irrationally, nay, in the strictest sense of the word, godlessly, or rather most irreverently, if we rejected that which is better, or did not help in advancing it, because in our short-sightedness we see difficulties heaping up a hundred years hence. My friend, it will take a long time for all the arable land in Europe to be dug up, planted, and weeded. It will be a still much longer time before Asia, Africa, and America will contain no more uncultivated paradises. At present, men, from indolence, prejudice, and foolish love for the corner in which they were born, do not want to emigrate thither. The Deity will compel them, through the expected higher enlightenment, to turn their attention to those districts as well, and thus, with the aid of the universal ennoblement, the whole earth will become a great garden of God, where one will joyfully observe on all sides the visible traces of human labor, whether of the hands or the head.

"A mass of former inhabitants of France are now settled in America. Fate drove them thither,—I say this from conviction,—and not accident. Who knows what important consequences this emigration will show in a few hundred years? For did not Richelieu accomplish a great deal of good in a short time at the Black Sea, both for Russia and for humanity? Famine drove two years ago a large number of Swiss to Russia and to America. So much the better, for there they will live more comfortably than at home, and will do much good."

He. "But when the earth will be filled with men, which will happen some day, what then?"

I. "My dear friend! This is one of the secrets or enigmas,—as you please—which the Deity has preserved for Himself, even as the preservation of the sexes in an equal proportion. With our present degree of education I consider it not only foolish, but even impudent, to try to pass any opinion on the matter. This is His affair!"

CHAPTER VI

Did I Intend to Make a Precocious Scholar Out of my Son?

I DID not mean to make a savant of him, much less a precocious scholar. This statement is absolutely true, but I shall not be surprised if it appears strange. and even unbelievable, to most readers.

But let me tell what I wanted to make of him; then it will appear of itself what I did not want him to become.

I wanted to educate him to be a man in the noblest sense of the word. So far as I in my circumstances could do so and was aided in this matter by my knowledge and experience, he was first of all to be a healthy, strong, active, and happy young man, and in this, as everybody knows, I have succeeded.

He was to enter manhood with this invaluable equipment. He was to develop his bodily powers to the utmost extent and yet harmoniously, even as he should do with his intellectual powers. It would have been in the highest degree unpleasant for me to have made of him pre-eminently a Latin or Greek scholar, or a mathematician. For this reason I immediately interfered whenever I thought that this or that language or science attracted him more than any other at too early a time.

The same I did with the strengthening and refining of his senses, which were exercised with care and developed as evenly as possible.

Aided by my wife, I proceeded in the same manner in the exercise of those powers which, alas! are only too seldom taken into consideration, such as common sense, power of imagination, delicacy of feeling, etc. Every sensible person, who has ripely considered what I have so far said, will himself understand that we, his parents, laid the chief weight on the education of the young heart, and that we worked together, from the time he was in his mother's arms, to regulate his likes and dislikes according to the laws of external and internal morality, more particularly according to the laws of the purest piety, and that some of these likes and dislikes had, therefore, to be repressed, while others were encouraged and promoted.

One will see that the picture which hovered before my mind's eye bore very little resemblance to the professional scholar of twenty years ago. It bears a somewhat closer resemblance to the scholar of to-day, and it may be hoped that in another twenty or fifty years the resemblance will be still closer.

Certainly the closet scholars of the time when I was considering the education of my future children,—I am speaking of the rule, for I have nothing to do with the memorable exceptions, whom I know and honor, —were chiefly sickly, weak, more dead than alive in life, and in society shy and awkward. Their external vision seldom went beyond the nearest books, and their internal vision not much farther than the science of their vocation. From this resulted that meager and dry conversation with any one who was not of their guild, and those shortsighted judgments about subjects of daily occurrence, by which they made themselves so despised and ridiculous among men of the world and refinement, so that it became a proverb with them to say, "He is as pedantic and helpless as a scholar," or, "You can notice ten steps away that he is a scholar." What an endless number of ridiculous incidents have arisen from it! It would be easy to fill a whole book with them.

The young man, who was considered a wit in society or who excelled with his gentler, refined sentiments and consequently despised the common, eternally recurring lecture-room passages, generally learned by heart or copied from somewhere, whose ennobled power of imagination made itself known by well-chosen, purely German, refined expressions in speaking and writing, at once fell under suspicion of those guildmen. More than once have I heard them express the judgment, "So and so cannot possibly have learned anything, for he writes verses and shines in society."

On the other hand, prolix, dry dissertations, with long, intricate periods, gained for an author, especially if he frequently quoted the old classics, the usual praise, "He will amount to something, for he has been trained on the ancients!"

The good ancients! How sarcastically

they would laugh, if they heard that such a housefly, such a bookworm, was compared with them, whose life from morning until evening passed in continuous action, in repeated conversations about the business of their fatherland or their paternal city, in the market or near the city gates!

Mind you, they were all essentially interested in the rise and fall of their fatherland, while those learned artisans frequently knew no more about it than that it existed.

One would hardly believe it that one of the greatest among those savants used to say to his students that Latin and Greek was the only thing that a sensible man needed to study, and that the so-called sciences (excluding the sciences of antiquity) and the modern languages were childish plays which one could conveniently study at the tea-table.

In regard to the heart I need only call to mind the well-known, almost classical expressions, "scholars' envy," "scholars' haughtiness," "university cabals," to be believed that I did not mean to make a professional scholar out of my son.

However, in so far as he had to become a scholar, he was at least not to be a precocious scholar, if I had anything to do with it. A precocious scholar, a hothouse plant, a sickly child, a child corpse, all these were to me, through my own experience, through my teachers, and through the great precursors in the art of education, identical terms. I should have regarded it a heavy transgression against God and against my son, if I had allowed myself to bring him up as a precocious scholar.

All I wanted to accomplish with my son was that in his seventeenth or eighteenth year he should be mature for the university, but that he should then have such a many-sided and thorough education as to be able to compete with any graduate, with the tacit conviction of his power to surpass them. That was all I wanted, and nothing more!

CHAPTER VII

HOW CAME MY SON TO BE A PRECOCIOUS SCHOLAR?

THAT happened quite naturally. If my friend Glaubitz, who knew me better than anybody, was right, it could not help happening. In spite of his mediocre aptitudes and in spite of my aversion against precocity, the foundation was laid through the education which he had received, and the results had to follow as surely as a ball must roll down an inclined plane once it has been placed at its upper end.

I did not recognize the fact then, for I was not sufficiently well acquainted with human nature, its powers, its perfectibility. I judged only from what I knew and what I saw all about me. Consequently my judgment could not help being wrong, and I had to study human nature more closely.

Oh, it stands very highly, much more highly than we imagine! But this is never seen under the so-called regular instruction. The usual method of education is a large, heavy dray which cannot pull itself from its deep ruts, or travel at a faster pace, and which, considering the many mediocre, or, to speak more correctly, the many ill-prepared minds, should not attempt to do otherwise.

These minds are like feeble itinerants, who walk by the side of the dray and have the more confidence in that dray, the slower and the more surely it advances. The poor fellows would be frightened out of their wits if it began to travel more rapidly, and the impotent ones would have to stay entirely behind, if it rushed away from them.

It is very different with a light, comfortable, safe vehicle. Without the use of many horses, it rushes with lightning rapidity past the creeping cart. But both, cart and carriage driver, would be very silly, if they despised one another, or made mutual recriminations. Both paces have their purposes and are adapted to circumstances. Both would act unnaturally, if they did differently. There may occur reasons why both would change their pace, but these rarely happen. The driver of the dray will travel more rapidly down a gentle incline, and his fellow-travelers will be able to keep up with him. In the deep sand, in the swamp, or among many rocks, the carriage will travel more slowly. All that is as it should be, and only a fool would want it to be otherwise.

Karl learned many things in the arms of his mother and in my own, such as one rarely thinks of imparting to children. He learned to know and name all the objects in the different rooms. The rooms themselves, the staircase, the yard, the garden, the stable, the well, the barn,—everything, from the greatest to the smallest, was frequently shown and clearly and plainly named to him, and he was encouraged to name the objects as plainly as possible. Whenever he spoke correctly, he was fondled and praised. When, however, he failed, we said in a decidedly cooler manner, "Mother (or Father), Karl cannot yet pronounce this or that word!"

Consequently he took great pains to know and correctly name all objects. Before long he pronounced all words, as we wanted him to do. There was no danger of stammering or stuttering, because he had to speak very slowly and was never intimidated. He thought and spoke freely, but he was obliged to think and to speak only after due consideration.

We did not tolerate that unwisdom of many parents and nurses, who begin by teaching the child a language, which they call baby talk, but which in reality should be called gibberish. No one was allowed to say "moo" instead of "cow," "bah" instead of "sheep," "meow" instead of "cat," "bow-wow" instead of "dog," nor "moo-cow, bah-sheep, meow-cat, bowwow-dog," but only "cow, sheep, cat, dog." The diminutives were permitted only in the case of young and small animals of the same species. If the word "doggy" was used, the reference was plainly to a young or very small dog. In the first case we intentionally varied it with the appellation "a very young dog," and remarked that that would be more correct. If it was small, but not exactly pretty, nor very young, we preferred to use the words "small dog" in place of "doggy," and directed his attention to the fact that the diminutive generally included the idea of prettiness and attractiveness on the part of the one so called, and of fondling on the part of the one calling it.

"When you have been naughty, that is, when you did not say or do what you should," we would say to him, "you will hardly hear us call you Karlchen. No, you are sure to be called Karl! Is it not so?"

We carefully observed this distinction, like many others of the kind, and in his company we always spoke pure German, in other words, book German, in very simple and comprehensible, but none the less choice expressions, and always loudly, distinctly, and in an appropriately slow manner. We never allowed ourselves to make an improper use of intonation. We spoke as correctly, in every sense of the word, as we could. Obscure and intricate sentences and expressions, such as gave no distinct meaning, were scrupulously avoided.

He had never heard, nor spoken, a confused childish babble, consequently there was no need for him to unlearn it and acquire a correct speech.

The only thing of the kind which I tolerated for a time was speaking in the third person, instead of using the abstract I, thou, he, etc., because it lies deeply in the nature of the uneducated man, consequently also of the child, not to be able easily to rise above it. This, however, took place only so long as it was unavoidable, whenever we wanted to be absolutely clear to him. Very soon we began to make the change, by using now and then the words "I, thou, he, she," for "father, mother, Karl," thus explaining one by the other, and preparing and facilitating the use of what was more correct. A little later, we jokingly, but with no bitterness whatsoever, would add, "If you were more intelligent, I should have said 'thou' (or 'I')."

Such a friendly jest, which refers to ignorance, want of intelligence, etc., urges the child on to make an effort and learn what he does not yet know.

In this manner Karl early learned to know and name correctly everything surrounding him, and what he could pronounce he always spoke in pure German, as though he had read it in a well-written book especially prepared for children. Indeed, he could not do otherwise, since he had never heard any bad German from us. He naturally enunciated his words so correctly and audibly that the little orator frequently evoked our smiles and strangers' admiration.

It is clear that the correct acquisition of his mother-tongue makes the child intelligent at an early time, for it puts his attention and his several mental powers continuously in action. He is obliged always to search, distinguish, compare, prefer, reject, choose, in short, he must work, that is, think. If he has proceeded correctly in this, he is praised. If he has made a mistake, he is jestingly reproved, or is given a helpful hint. He then once more goes through his mental processes, is happier, and rejoices at his struggle and victory, as also at the paternal or maternal approval.

Besides, how useful it is for memory! If the above-mentioned activities are to take place, there is need of a supply of words, hence memory must be active, to grasp and keep them. Let us assume that of the enormous treasure of the German language only thirty thousand words pass into the child's mind in his first five or six years, and this may be easily accomplished in the case of an exceptionally well-brought-up child. See the chance memory has in that case to be exercised and strengthened! And how the child is at the same time urged on, if he has been accustomed to it and feels the inclination to speak with reflection and care! With but very little aid the child sketches for himself a kind of grammar and, according to his ability, likes to pick out the various changes of nouns and verbs. It is only then that he invites the beneficent aid of real grammar, be it from the mouth of his father, or in a printed book, if he has become accustomed to reading.

All this has been vaguely felt before, hence instruction began with the ancient languages. Unfortunately it was felt only vaguely, otherwise the inexcusable thing would not have happened of neglecting the mother tongue and intimidating the child's mind by the dry dead languages, and thus choking his intellect in the germ.

This early occupation with the mother tongue introduced Karl every day more and more into its inner depths, and prepared him for learning the foreign languages with great facility.

What under other conditions would have disgusted or frightened him in these languages was now, indeed, new, but not entirely strange to him. He had learned something like it in his mother tongue, and had made it his own. All he had to do was to modify something, and the strange language was clear to him. As he had accustomed himself to do mental work, such occupation gave him pleasure, for he knew full well that every struggle brought with it a victory, and that victory was enjoyable.

The natural consequence of all that was that he, without great effort, read in the original Homer, Plutarch, Virgil, Cicero, Ossian, Fénelon, Florian, Metastasio, and Schiller, and that, too, with sincere pleasure, often with true enthusiasm, when he was but eight years old. Therefore the great linguist Heyne of Goettingen sixteen months later said of him in writing that he was possessed of a sagacity, common only to able minds, of guessing correctly what he did not know. Heyne, no doubt, was right, for he had examined him very carefully among thousands whom he had examined before, and I would have said that my method of education was a failure, if it had not been thus. But here are Heyne's own words to Wieland:

GOETTINGEN, *July* 25, 1810.

REVERED VETERAN:

Pastor Dr. Witte spoke to me with grateful praise of your good wishes and plans for his son's further education.

Although I am not a friend of precocious maturity, and respect the common laws of Nature, I also recognize that Nature herself makes exceptions, and that it becomes our duty to take her hints and further the early development of a more capable mind. In that respect and in order more closely to study the boy's aptitudes and natural ability, with a view to a possible wider development, for the boy's own sake and advantage, I allowed myself to be persuaded to observe him nearer at hand, and by an examination to form my own judgment, independently from other people's judgments and from admirers; not merely for the purpose of observing him as a product of Nature, fit for experiments, but also in order to determine whether it would be possible to make of him, through an education adapted to his natural aptitudes, a happy, humanly and civilly useful member of society,—which, indeed, might not be an easy task.

I found the boy hale and hearty in body and mind, more than I had expected. I tried him with Homer and Virgil, and I found that he possessed sufficient verbal and material information to translate readily and get the sense,—a natural ability, generally possessed by capable minds, without a more exact grammatical or logical knowledge, to guess the context correctly. The most remarkable thing to me was that he read sensibly, with feeling and effect. Otherwise I found in him no other preponderating mental power, no striking talent: memory, imagination, intelligence were at about a balance. In other things, such as were not drilled in by instruction, I found him to be a happy, hale boy, not even averse to mischief, which was a consolation to me. As to his predilection for epic poets and earnest, soul-stirring poems and writings, his previous education may account for that,—a notable testimony to his father's way of bringing him up.

We shall hardly live long enough to see the final results of the method employed, but I heartily hope, like yourself, that the State, as we are wont to say, will take advantage of the uncommon favor of Nature, and that the boy may some day attain a commensurate degree of happiness. To judge from appearances, his vocation, usefulness, and good fortune will lie in the field of learning, perhaps more especially in that of history.

Pardon me, revered friend, for having expatiated at greater length than I had intended to. I was therein misled by the pleasure of conversing with you once more.

Devotedly yours,
HEYNE.

When still a small child, of four or five years, Karl derived an incredible amount of profit from his thorough knowledge of his mother tongue. He had not acquired it from dead books, in the manner in which Greek and Latin are usually funneled into children, and, alas, in the opinion of many men still living, must be funneled in, or rather beaten in.

Sixteen hours of Latin a week for a thirteen-year-old boy! That is bad, and I unfortunately am speaking of the year 1818 and of a famous school at Berlin.

Karl learned his pure German rather in life, in the house, in the garden, in the meadow, field, and forest, in society, on long and short journeys, in short, under all the various conditions which I in my situation was able to create for him. In his first year we began to take him with us wherever we went, and, as far as possible, he had everything explained to him, especially if he seemed to be attracted by anything.

Thus he had in the first two years of his life accompanied us to Merseburg, Halle, Leipsic, Weissenfels, Naumburg, Dessau, Woerlitz, Wittenberg, etc., and in all these places he learned a mass of things which he would never have seen at home.

In his third and fourth years he still more frequently visited those places, received better impressions of what he had seen and heard there, grasped it more clearly, and expanded his circle of knowledge. He naturally saw more important and more interesting things, for in his third year he passed eight weeks in Leipsic, and in his fourth and fifth he went with me to Magdeburg, Halberstadt, Salzwedel, Stendal, the Mannsfeld territory, a part of the Harz Mountains, etc. He was introduced into every kind of society and to everything memorable He, consequently, was as well acquainted with the concert, drama, and opera, as with watermills and windmills, with lions, ostriches, and elephants, as with moles and bats, with salt mines as with steam engines, with the village market as with the Leipsic Fair, with excavations as with mines, with brilliant society as with a poor day-laborer's cabin, with the dancing-floor as with the death-bed.

None of these things he knew by merely staring at them, as children generally know them, but thoroughly, often more thoroughly than adults know them, for his mother and I every time discussed the matters with him, or, purposely, with each other in his presence. He was frequently asked whether he had taken good notice of this or that, and how he had liked it. He soon became accustomed to repeating and discussing what he had seen and heard, and he himself addressed us, inquired, reported, retorted, etc.

If one considers that in his fifth year he

traveled with me to Potsdam and Berlin, through Priegnitz and by many roads through Mecklenburg as far as Rostock, Warnemuende, and Dobberan, that he went to sea in still weather and in moderate storms, that he observed commerce and navigation, then proceeded over Ludwigslust to the Altmark, and here for weeks lived in the country, in all kinds of social circles and districts, everywhere considered and treated as a beloved child of their own, that people took real delight in the little questioner and babbler, and readily gave him every desired information,—one will easily understand that he thus laid by a treasure of linguistic and material information, such as but few older persons possess.

I must lay special stress on this that he knew nothing wrongly, nothing in a prejudiced way, in so far as we, his parents, knew the objects correctly. If we lacked the precise information, we had ourselves and Karl instructed by the best-trained and best instructed men.

In his sixth year I passed with him six weeks in Dresden, thoroughly acquainted him with the beautiful nature of the place and of its surroundings, especially with its many art treasures, and, by constant observation and repeated discussions about them, which we had then and later, improved his taste. While in Leipsic, Potsdam, and Berlin, or wherever anything beautiful was to be seen, I had begun to guard him against the childish delight in bright-colored pictures, the drawing of which was wrong. He was particularly cautioned against it during our visits to the Dresden Art Gallery, particularly to the inner Italian Hall, among the antiques and Mengs' casts. Since then I have never noticed in him any silly judgments about matters of art, such as one too frequently hears, even from grown children!

As soon as the weather became settled, during our stay in Dresden, we visited the Plauischer Grund, Tharand, and the whole Saxon Switzerland. Since I had previously and more than once seen everything beautiful there, with a book in my hand and a guide at my side, nothing was then overlooked or carelessly inspected. What variety these heavenly regions offer to the adult, and still more to a child of six years! The lovely surroundings of Schandau and Lohmen, the

Liebethaler and the Ottowalder Grund, the Kuhstall and the Prebischthor, the Bastion, the basaltic columns at Stolpe, and the high Winterberg, finally the Koenigstein, Lilienstein, Sonnenstein, and Pillnitz.

All the above objects, and many more, were correctly named to Karl, and we spoke, read, and passed opinions concerning them. Our guides, friends, and acquaintances shared their sentiments with him and with me. He told it all to his mother and his young and old friends in Merseburg, Halle, and Leipsic, and wrote about it to distant acquaintances. He thus had it entirely in his power to express himself intelligently and clearly about it.

The useful result of this is much greater than one may think, for the more objects a man knows correctly, with their names and properties, and the better he can impart that knowledge to others, the greater is the mental supply which he has laid in and over which he has command, and the more frequently he finds himself induced "to seek, compare, distinguish, prefer, reject, or choose—that is, to work, to think;" and the more a man thinks, the more he learns to think. Consequently there is an immeasurable gain, if we can get the children first to think before they want to do or say something.

A child that is accustomed to think learns every moment more and more. It may be that the particular subject is too difficult for him at the time being, but having become used to wanting to understand it (I would say of the properly educated child "to being obliged to understand it"), he at least tries to retain what he cannot understand, and, without knowing it himself, quietly works at it, in order to make clear to himself what so far has been obscure to him. He inquires, investigates, listens to something that bears a relation to it. He may be reading about an entirely different matter, but he finds some hint, some elucidation, which seems to him to refer to that which he did not understand before. Now all his mental powers are put into new activity. He reads on industriously, quizzes his parents, teachers, friends, playmates,—in short, he does not rest until, plowing his way through the unsteady waves of ignorance, he arrives at the firm, blossoming shore of clear insight.

Significant also is the observation that a child that has at an early time become acquainted with many things, has become familiar with their names and properties, and has with ease and correctness expressed himself about them, will very attentively listen to the conversation of adults. He will not find it tiresome, will not yawn during it, will not behave with stupid, childish attention, that is, with thoughtlessness. As he understands the greater part of it, he will take sincere interest in it. If there is something that he does not understand, his interest will thereby be increased, for what is said is new to him, he wants to and must understand it, and his habitual activity will not rest, until this knot, too, has been untied.

What an immeasurable amount a child will learn in six, eight, or ten years, that is, in 3,650 days, in 36,500 hours, reckoning the day at ten hours, if every conversation with him or in his presence teaches him something!

It is on this that my firm conviction is based that even a mediocre child may be approximated to a higher being, if one understands how to do it, and is able and willing to try it.

CHAPTER VIII

Did I Pretend to have the Necessary Skill for Making a Scholar of my Son?

Oh, no! I had, indeed, in schools and universities done as well as the best around me, and as a graduate I had constantly and most carefully attended to my higher education, as is attested by the various learned examinations which I passed before Chaplain Kletzke, in the Consistory at Magdeburg, and in the Higher Consistory at Berlin. Nor had I ceased instructing others, consequently I had added to my knowledge. I had, besides, been, with a kindness which put me to shame, offered teaching positions in the institutions of the then greatest educators of Germany, Gedike, Salzmann, Pfeffel, Karoline Rudolphi, etc. Yet I considered it unthinkable for a single person, with a very moderate income, living in the country, without possessing any means for instruction or being able to provide them promptly, to carry the education of a rapidly and well-progressing child any farther than to his eighth or tenth year—that is, as I then thought, until he would be able to attend the lowest of the upper divisions of a higher institution of learning.

I, therefore, planned, before and after Karl's birth, for men like Gedike and Schewe to take active part in his upbringing, as soon as I should no longer be able to give him the proper instruction. In their institutions there were ten or twelve teachers, and in the Grey Cloister at Berlin there were possibly even more. With the funds at their disposal they could choose the ablest candidates, and appoint them to such branches of instruction as they felt them to be most fitted for. I considered all that, and so I was far from imagining that I should be able to take their place.

Just as during the education of my son there showed themselves a few evil men who tried to crush what I and my friends were planting, so there will be found some even now who will say, "That is nothing but assumed modesty! He certainly had the confidence that he would be able to accomplish what he wanted to accomplish, and, possibly, even more."

I must expect something like that, to judge from the malicious, secret doings of certain gentlemen who in time will be found out and treated with contempt, for those who are capable of doing something bad to a distinctly good cause are obliged to defend or, at least, mantle their meanness. The method which these gentlemen employed was, with the aid of their henchmen, good friends, clients, and disciples, to circulate a mass of calumnies, now orally in the town, now by letters to the outside world, now by articles and reviews in periodicals of every description.

All that was done with great slyness, doing my son and me harm, but the tricksters have not attained their ends, for my son is still respected and loved.

The good cause is well established and, with God's aid, will become yet better established. Should my son or I soon pass into a better world, the proof will have been given, none the less, that man's education can, without doing him injury, proceed much more rapidly than has heretofore been supposed.

I take up the expected objection that I had the confidence of accomplishing what I have accomplished, and I reply, "No!" My preparations at the child's birth show that I am telling the truth. My later behavior proves it still more clearly.

As soon as my son had made some progress in Latin and was to begin Greek, I looked about for a teacher to help me, because I felt that I could not do what should be done in accordance with my ideal.

In Halle, in Leipsic, in Magdeburg, in Berlin, everywhere I tried, at the sacrifice of what for me was a very great yearly salary and excellent upkeep, to get the kind of man I wanted to have, but fate was against me. What I wanted only a very few could do, and these few had more advantageous situations or such as offered them better prospects for the future.

I wanted a man who could read Greek as easily and with as much pleasure as I could read German, Latin, Italian, or French; who, at the same time, would be such a master of his mother-tongue as to be able with little exertion to render every Greek expression into German; who with just as little exertion could correctly translate back into Greek and would know all the grammatical forms, even for all the dialects, and could deduce them from one another,—in short, a man who, in company with the boy, could sketch a short Greek grammar. It was still more important for me that he should be thoroughly acquainted with the whole of Greek literature and with the people to whom it belonged, with Greece, Magna Græcia, Asia Minor, the islands, with all the countries at the different periods of Greek culture. At the same time he should know their constitutions, governments, customs, habits, usages, entertainments, life in peace and in war, their education, morals, religion, law, politics, commerce, arts and sciences. I should have been still more pleased if he had been as well acquainted with Rome and with everything that goes with it.

I thought I had found such a man in my former schoolmate, Dr. B., and through our common friend Glaubitz I made proposals to him which meant great monetary sacrifices for me. But, as he told us, he had already committed himself to a situation which he was obliged to keep as an honest man, and which from considerations of advantage, he did not wish to give up.

Many others had been recommended to me,

before and after him, but most of them, upon closer acquaintance, appeared useless for my purpose; indeed, most did not possess as much knowledge of the two languages as I had. Still less were they capable of fulfilling the higher demands.

I shall relate one case, for the rest are very much alike.

A graduate student from our part of the country returned with much acclaim from the university. He himself, his parents, and his relatives assured all that he had been the favorite student of one of our greatest philologists. He was proposed to me with the assurance that I should be very fortunate if he decided to become my assistant.

His boastful statements, of which I had heard, made me distrustful. I, therefore, replied that I was just then undecided as to what I was going to do, but that I should be very happy if Mr. W.—that was his name—would for a week leave his parents, in order to stay with me, and would daily instruct my son for half an hour in Greek according to my method.

I purposely let him the first day watch how I acted during the instruction, after I had expounded my ideas to him. The next morning his teaching began. I had asked him to begin with one of the easy readers, which I had procured; but he entered the room with the Iliad in his hand, and forthwith proceeded to deliver himself of a very scholarly introduction which I was compelled to believe he had merely learned by heart. In this supposition I was strengthened by the blunders and startling lacunæ in the context.

Karl would now and then utter a sigh, and looked at him as at some strange animal, which one was more afraid of than glad to see. Occasionally the boy would open his mouth, as if to say, "I do not understand a word of it all!" but that was quite in vain, for the torrent of Mr. W.'s eloquence immediately closed it again.

The boy stood it all patiently, and so did I.

When the half hour was over, but the learned introduction had not yet come to an end, I asked him to close it for the day, and to take up five minutes in translation. This I would prefer to be made from the reader, or, if Mr. W. so chose it, from the Iliad.

Mr. W. began to translate from the Iliad. He scanned every verse with great pathos, and poured forth a translation in such an impure, now and then execrable, German that I was simply horrified. My poor little son was overcome with terror, for he thought, from his previous experience, that I would demand of him readily to repeat what he had heard.

I, therefore, at once freed him from his fear, by saying, with a merry jest, "My dear boy, you cannot repeat that, for it is as yet too learned for you! For you to be able to repeat it well, you have to get it translated in company with the teacher. That could not be done here, because Mr. W. knows his Homer too well, and so does not have to look up in the dictionary and grammar, as I do with you. It would be bothersome for him, but I do it gladly out of love for you, as you know."

That quieted Karl and did not hurt Mr. W. When we were left alone, I asked him to come down from his high pitch, because otherwise Karl would derive no profit from his instruction. But he asserted that that was the proper way to teach, and that he had faithfully copied his great teacher.

"Excuse me," I replied, "that is so much the worse, for I am not at all sure that this way is proper for youths, and I certainly am convinced that it is quite useless for a child of seven years."

He insisted he was right, and he was my guest, so I suffered patiently and merely asked him to consider my son's weakness and my sincere wish, and to instruct Karl the next day from one of the Greek readers at hand. At last he unwillingly promised to do so. None the less the next day he terrified Karl and me by his Homer.

Having listened to him in suffering for fifteen minutes, I interrupted him very earnestly:

"Karl," said I, "do you understand what Mr. W. lectures to you? That is, do you understand it sufficiently well to be able to recite it to me?"

The poor boy, who had never been in such a painful situation before, said, with a deep sigh:

"No, dear father, I cannot do that! Much of it I do not understand, and the rest I have not listened to."

"Well," I replied, "then I ask you most earnestly, Mr. W., to put the Iliad aside and to take this reader. I thank you very much for your good will, but Karl, as you see, is still too far behind to be able to grasp Homer. I am sure you wish to be useful to him and obliging to me."

After many objections and assurances that it would all come out well in the end, that Karl would every day understand him better, etc., he finally made up his mind to do what he could not avoid, that is, to translate the first little story in the reader with Karl.

The great, superior learning at once came to an end. There occurred words and forms which embarrassed him, and as he was too vain to look them up, he was satisfied to guess at them and to translate the whole with approximate correctness and—in bad German.

All that was so contrary to my intentions that I repeatedly requested him to go slowly and to render word for word exhaustively. Karl, too, asked him to do so, but in vain. I, therefore, put an end to the whole matter by showing him that Karl had hardly understood a thing in the story which he had been reading to him. I translated the next story to him in my own way, and Karl was aglow with joy and could hardly wait to translate the story to us. When he had to do that, he had complete command of it, and, in spite of all objections and quizzing questions on my part, he rendered it almost the way I had translated it to him the first time.

Anybody but a Moor would have been washed white by such an experience, but Mr. W. was too puffed up to be able to doubt his knowledge or power of teaching. I no longer troubled him with the instruction, and in a few days he left us altogether.

I have unfortunately had several such experiences and have seen and heard of many more. How a poor child is to be pitied that falls into the hands of such a man!

He not only learns next to nothing, but, what is much worse, his head is being filled with incorrect notions, which later on hinder him in seeing and acquiring what is correct. He becomes accustomed to wander about with half-grasped ideas, and to consider the teacher who has imparted them to him as a light of the world and, like his model, to despise his betters who bring and demand clearness in everything. "That man has no learning! He knows only what is comprehensible to everybody," that is what his admired teacher has meant to say only too often, and the boy has ended by blabbing it after him. His ideas about studying, learning, and scholars will, in consequence, remain wrong, possibly for all time, as we only too often hear grown-ups deliver such misjudgments.

Much worse are the evil consequences of such instruction upon life. The boy does not learn anything in a proper manner, grasps nothing clearly, receives nothing as his possession, but by degrees allows the half-truths or even the absolute nonsense to be funneled into him, babbles the undigested stuff, and considers himself to be a wiseacre, if his superficialities can surprise and perplex others as his teacher perplexed him before. Then he proceeds to act in the same way in all the affairs of life.

He considers it common and low to insist on clear, enlightening views, or to respect and emulate those who have them. He can never master his subject completely, for he has not been taught how to do this. Nor would he wish to master it, for he feels at home in the half-darkness, and fears the clear light of common-sense.

Hence the opinion entertained concerning scholars of that type is frequently correct, when it is said of them that they are not fit for affairs, for they stir up the clear water until it becomes turbid. They heap rocks upon rocks in order to level a molehill, but they only cover it and make the evil so much the worse.

Worst of all are the consequences of such confusing instruction upon the heart. I have found that the men of that class are usually very conceited and extremely supercilious toward persons with brighter views,—if they do not fear them or expect something from them. And as the faults of the parents and teachers are easily transferred to the children and pupils, there is danger that even these will be transmitted to the younger generation.

After many failures I finally came to the conclusion that my nearest friends, for example Professor W., Pastor Glaubitz, and others, might be right when they asserted that I possessed the necessary knowledge to advance my son farther than I had dared to hope.

However, they were not entirely right, although the start seemed to justify them, for they had counted too little upon the perfectibility of human nature, which is immeasurably great.

Had I been obliged to impart everything to my son in the usual way, I should not have been able to bring him half so far as I actually have brought him, and I should have wasted two or three times the energy and time and have caused him a considerable amount of torture. But I proceeded in the very opposite direction, and he would have learned a great deal more, if I had known more of the subject.

He learned constantly, without noticing it. He increased, refined, and heightened his mental powers to such an extent that he soon saw through every subject that presented itself to him; or, at least, did all he could in order to see through it, for

"His wings with the victory grew!"

Yet he did not imagine that he was doing anything but what any child, any ordinary man, did and should do. Besides, he learned gladly because he experienced manifold pleasures in doing so, and observed the constant growth of his ability to advance still farther.

While so many people get tired of studying and learning, he became ever more eager for it. It actually caused him torment to discover a field of knowledge in which he knew little or nothing. "Oh, how much pleasure I am missing!" he would not only say, but also feel, with tears of longing. Hence his immeasurably high respect for those who knew more than he, and the tender gratitude which he showed a person who gave himself the trouble to enlighten him.

He seized every book, every science, every language with the eager desire of making its excellent contents his own. When such a state is reached with boys and youths, everything has been attained. The rest is done by God, or, rather, by the power which he gives, the divine spark, which, unobserved by the common eye, glows very brightly within us.

A boy who has been thus guided advances farther and farther, until impeded by the limitations of human or his own particular nature. He will and must attain to something high and good.

I surmised all this, but I only surmised it. I did not see it as clearly and as surely as later on. But I grasped it with sufficient clearness, to base an idea upon it which was at once received in Leipsic with universal approval. I resolved, with the encouragement of my late friend, Professor Erhard, to open an educational institution which would give its pupils the kind of preparation my son had received.

I intended to take in this preparatory school no more than ten children at a time, in order to give them the best personal attention, and I intended to select and educate my own teachers, and to guide as much as possible in person, in order to minimize annoyances. It was evident what I wanted to accomplish, and people were quite satisfied with the probable results, and they had confidence in my necessary power and sufficient will. They offered me boys on all sides, and as young as I wanted them, and all other offers were satisfactory to me. I could not yet take boarding pupils, and so was to take them as half-boarders.

My wife, too, was requested to do the same with ten girls, and she was also offered children from the best families under the same conditions. But Fate willed otherwise, for the Westphalian Government ordered me to go with my son to Goettingen. I was thus obliged to reject those offers and the stipend for my son at Leipsic, but I will all my life think gratefully of the proffered kindness.

Now I know human perfectibility still better. Now I am positive that such a preparatory school would suffice to educate the children's bodies, minds, and souls to such an extent that their powers in all three directions would soon appear unusually great and they would be able to withstand evil influences from without; that the mental powers of children so educated would above all put them in a position to work their own way and, with only mediocre further instruction, accomplish extraordinary results in the world. For, once the powers of the human soul have had the proper incitement, they can never be repressed afterward. Put fetters upon them, and they will break them and come out still more powerful. Men whose mental powers have once been awakened and later repressed, have often unexpectedly trodden new paths, on which they have accomplished incredible results. Decidedly, it will long remain an unsolved riddle where human perfectibility ends,—so far are we, according to my sincere conviction, still removed from the goal.

CHAPTER IX

Objections to the Early Education of my Son

It is impossible to relate all the objections which reason and unreasonableness, kindness of heart and meanness, have brought forward. I touch only upon those that seem to be sensible, and, therefore, have remained in my memory. I will refute them as briefly as possible.

I must distinctly mention here that the main objections emanated from people who had not yet met the boy. As a rule they took everything back as soon as they saw and spoke with him.

When he was eight years old, he became known to the world of scholars.

"He must be sickly and feeble," they said, "and the gain of early maturity is as nothing in comparison with the child's health."

Excellent men, who knew the child intimately, testified over their names that he was perfectly well.

"He will grow sick in his ninth or tenth

year, then he will drag out a sickly year or two, and will die in the eleventh or twelfth year of his brief existence."

He neither grew ill nor died.

"He, no doubt, passes most of his time at the study-table, and that cannot be good for him!"

Men, who knew better, made public declaration that he passed less time at the table studying than almost any child.

"He does not enjoy his childhood!"

Others,—not I,—were loud in asserting that it would not be easy to find a happier and a merrier child.

"He is too much left to himself!"

Yet it became daily better known that I used to take him with me while he was still a mere infant, and introduced him into all kinds of society.

"He will grow too serious!"

To this the highest authorities testified that upon occasion, when it was required, he could become very serious, but that the moment that was no longer necessary, he was childishly happy, nay, could be wanton and naughty, just as any well-brought-up child may be.

"Children's amusements must annoy him!"

Guthsmuths and others went on record as affirming that he took active part in all the games of children, and gamboled about and played with children with visible joy.

"He will never know how to get along with children!"

Children who became acquainted with him would rather play with him than with any other child, because he demanded nothing unreasonable of them, did not spoil their things, and yielded pleasantly.

"He will be proud, vain, self-willed, and will look down contemptuously upon his playmates!"

His playmates stopped envying him his knowledge, and tolerated the respect and love which he, on that account, enjoyed from their parents and other relatives, only because he was so modest and unpretentious, and not infrequently tried to learn from them what they knew better than he.

He never paraded his knowledge, and there could be no thought of boasting.

"He is being educated just for the study-table, and so he will feel himself out of place in society, and will not know how to behave there."

But he was liked as much at court as in peasants' cabins, in the house of the wealthy merchant as of the minister, in the society of the refined landed proprietor as of the honest burgher, all insisted that he fitted into their circle as though he had been brought up for it.

"In his thirteenth to fifteenth year, when he reaches the age of puberty, he will grow weak, will fade away and die!"

All that did not happen, but, on the contrary, he grew very strong, blossomed like a rose, and continued to live.

"If he survives that critical period and carries away no bodily harm, he will none the less be mentally affected. He will stand still, and of what use will it then be that he formerly advanced so rapidly."

He was not mentally affected, but kept making rapid progress as before.

"He will have a mind for nothing but learning and dry languages. What is beautiful and pleasing will forever remain a matter of indifference to him. What an irretrievable loss for him!"

Indeed, indeed, if it were only true! But even as a child did he love the beautiful in

Nature, in the world of man and beast, as well as in the works of the great authors and poets, and he was quick in finding and pointing it out. Later on he recited and read exceptionally well, as most cultured people asserted. For that reason and because of the joy with which he took part in social games, or directed them, he was much sought for in elegant society, and especially by young men and women of refinement.

Now he writes both prose and poetry with indescribable ease and, as I am assured, not without success.

The last objection which I shall mention came from St. Petersburg. It was the only one which for a time perplexed me, because it referred to too remote a future for me to be able to refute it by anything in the present. And yet I did not dare to present the future all too favorably to myself. Besides, the objection came from one whom I respected equally as a philosopher and as a sensible, experienced, and well-meaning man, who loved me and mine, and communicated his misgivings to me in confidence, without trying maliciously to set the world of scholars against me and my work.

Kollegienrath von Jakob, formerly my teacher as Professor of Philosophy at Halle, later my friend and baptismal witness of my last child, wrote me under July 23, 1811, when Karl was eleven years old, as follows:

As regards your son, I can easily understand how such a child may cause his parents great pleasure, which is the more agreeable to me, since these parents are my friends, whom I love. Yet I must confess to you that my pleasurable sensation has not been without an admixture of regret, for I am not yet convinced that this marvelous precocity will be an advantage to your child, from which he will be happier and more perfect than other men. I am certainly convinced that your skill and endeavor are mainly responsible for the early development of the child's powers. Just as certain it appears to me that your son has extraordinary natural gifts, which willingly follow the incitement of the paternal instruction.

But if this early development is to give your son lasting advantages, it must proceed proportionately. The power and knowledge which your son has received up to his ninth or eleventh year, another young man of talent attains only in his fifteenth to nineteenth year. The increase of mental powers generally takes place up to one's twenty-first year, after which knowledge and experience may be added, but hardly a greater reasoning power. If now your son's reasoning power continues to increase in the same proportion from his ninth to his twenty-first year, he will indisputably stand out for the rest of his life as a very exceptional man. But let us assume that the degree of his reasoning becomes fixed in his fourteenth year. If so, he will in his twenty-first year be no further advanced than other men of his age, except, perhaps, that he will have some more knowledge. Your son would, then, be admired up to his eighteenth or twentieth year, after which he would all of a sudden be reckoned among the class of all other men.

I now must submit to your consideration the effect which the continued admiration of what is extraordinary in him, which cannot help affecting him, must produce upon him, and what his sensations will be, if in his twentieth or twenty-first year he sees the admiration vanish and finds himself counted among ordinary men. This consideration would fill me with great anxieties, if I were the child's father. A man who has exercised public attention from his childhood, must feel it hard when he is no longer so highly regarded. Those, my dear friend, are my misgivings in regard to the educational system which you have chosen. You know that I am in the habit always to express my thoughts freely and openly, and I especially like to do so toward persons whom I respect and love.

I answered him before long, saying that what he was afraid of might be true, but that I, for good reasons, had no such fear, and that I would use the proper precaution, so that it would not harm Karl much, if, indeed, it should happen: that three years hence, at my son's fourteenth year, I would write him (Professor von Jakob) openly and honestly, as is my wont, about further developments. If his misgivings came true I would not hide it from him, but, in the contrary case, he must allow me to announce the truth to him in my name and in the name of my son.

On June 22, 1814, when my son was within ten days of fourteen years, I wrote him as follows:

But first of all concerning your opinion of my son! Your idea that the degree of his intellect might become fixed in his fourteenth year and he would not advance any further, therefore would cease being admired in his twentieth or twenty-first year and so would become ill-tempered, is exceedingly clever; and I must confess to you that no other man made that objection to me, wherefore it at first perplexed me very much. I am one of those few who do not try to reason away what at a future day may cause them an unpleasantness. It may be that things will happen as you think, but so far it does not seem likely. (1) My son will be fourteen years old on the first of July, and he is still visibly gaining in intellectual powers. (2) He is still extremely modest, and does not wish to be admired, or, rather, does not notice that he is admired.

I, therefore, hope that he will not so soon come to a standstill, or that, if it occurs, he will grieve less than would a vain young man about the cessation of admiration, so that nothing will be lost, whereas much will be won—a careful education, a mass of information, early experiences, knowledge of the world, acquaintance with refined society through his travels and through the respectful and kind reception accorded him in the best homes.

Neither of us can decide the matter,—it lies "in the

lap of the blessed gods," but probability is much more on my side now than three years ago.

Thus this last objection, which, for the reasons mentioned, caused me more anxiety than any other, has been happily overcome. Thank Heaven, if I had to answer that letter to-day, I would do it with greater calm and with more joyful gratitude toward God, for what I wrote on that twenty-second of June is as fully true to-day as then. Indeed, it seems to me that I could now say more for me and my son.

CHAPTER X

Did my Son Profit from his Early Education?

Certainly! And in many essential ways.

One of the main foundations of his education was training for piety and morality. He saw in everything God,—his Father and the Father of all. He honored and loved everything about him, down to beasts and plants, as his fellow-creatures, consequently to some extent as his brothers and sisters. He, therefore, strove to stand higher and higher on the great ladder of gradations, but without any envy and contempt for other beings. On the contrary, he respected them sincerely and loved them tenderly. He had deep compassion for those whom he thought to be under him. He endeavored to raise himself only through the instruction of his parents, through intercourse with cultured people, and through his own industry, and all those means were dear to him, quite contrary to the manner of ordinary children.

He spoke with God as with his friend, thanked Him for His gifts and His kindly guidance, asked for His further aid in his affairs and referred every agreeable occurrence, every pleasure which he enjoyed, to Him, the All-good, the giver of joys. In the harmonica, as in the blossoming rose; in Raphael's painting, as in the song of the thrush; in the mountains of Saxon Switzerland, as in the blade of grass; in spiritual man, as in the cleverness of his dog—everywhere he saw and felt God.

He prayed often and eagerly, but preferably when left alone, or in the presence of only his parents, reluctantly before a third person. That one may be able to judge his manner of praying, I communicate a prayer which, in its fundamental idea, I have frequently heard him recite. But he prayed differently in the different conditions and situations of life. If we were on the point of traveling, he begged God to protect us further, and thanked Him for His previous aid. If we were somewhere visiting, he prayed God richly to reward our friends for their kindness, and so forth. If one of us, his parents, or his friends, was ill, he prayed for his recovery. Here is the general scheme of it:

Karl's Heartfelt Prayer, Evening and Morning, with Variations, According to Times and Circumstances

"I thank you, O God, for having given us such a good night. Give us also a good day! Reward my parents for the good education which they have given me heretofore! Help them to continue to give it to me in the future! Preserve them for me safe and sound for a long time to come! Thanks for the many joys which I have daily been enjoying through them and through other men! Assist me to-day to be well-behaved, obedient, and diligent! Make me choose a vocation which will be the most useful for me and for my parents!

"Keep me from avarice, pride, impure thoughts, and lying! Give us the pleasant, if it is salutary for us! Give us also that which seems evil to us, if it is good for us, even if we ask you to avert it from us! Teach us to bear wrongs! Reward those who have done much for me! Be good to all men, especially to those who suffer!"

This principle of a pious and moral education, the detailed acquaintance with what is most instructive in the Old, and especially in the New Testament, most of all with the life and teachings of Jesus, in the best extracts and writings, laid a very solid foundation for his future rectitude and kindness of heart. The contemplation of the Deity in all His creations, the frequent, intimate conversation with Him, kept his own constant attention upon himself, so that he did not easily allow himself to do any wrong or to be led into it by anybody else. His heart was and remained so innocent that very sensible people called him as pure as an angel.

For that reason he would do nothing in our absence that he was forbidden to do. He would say that God sees it all and should not be offended. Occurrences of the kind I am going to relate were common and, in the nature of things, had to happen.

We were once visiting Pastor E. at L. Next morning, at the coffee-drinking, Karl carelessly spilled some of his milk on the table.

The law was that in such a case he was to be punished by getting nothing more to eat or drink, except bread and salt.

He was very fond of milk. The E.'s had on that occasion made it particularly sweet for him and had given him a piece of fine cake with it, because they had become exceedingly fond of him. Karl suddenly grew purple in his face, was very much embarrassed, and stopped drinking. I knew well why, but I pretended I did not see it.

The E.'s, too, saw it, and encouraged him to finish his milk. He declined, and finally admitted that he could not go on drinking, because he had carelessly spilled some on the table. They naturally assured him that that did not make any difference, and that he should go on drinking his milk. I kept quiet, and purposely busied myself with picking up our things. Karl could not be moved, so that the E.'s finally, from their great love for the child, grew angry at me, because they imagined that I had given him the command by a nod.

I then sent Karl out, and explained to them how it all was. But there was no use. They insisted that it was against nature for a healthy child, who had a good appetite, to decline sweet milk with cake, because a law forbade him to do so, on account of a little transgression.

"Just go away, and he will drink his milk!"

"Very well," I replied, "I will go away, in order that you may see that his behavior flows from his soul and is not forced by me, but on the one condition that you later tell me the whole truth, how it has all happened. I promise you in advance that I will not reprove him if he should drink the milk."

They promised me that they would tell me all about it.

Now Karl was called in, and I went away under some pretext. The E.'s did their best to make him eat and drink, but in vain. They sweetened his milk still more. But that did no good. They told him that they would fill up the cup as before, so that I should not notice the difference, and they offered him other cake, with the sophical remark, "The law cannot forbid this!" They particularly directed his attention to the fact that I should not find out anything about it. Karl remained unperturbed, and he repeated:

"Even if my father does not know it, God

does, and that is the main thing. It would certainly be a deception if I should partake of other milk and cake."

They reminded him that he had to take a long walk and that he needed the proper sustenance for it. He insisted that bread and salt made red cheeks, and would give him the required strength.

They finally saw themselves obliged to call me in, and they told me, with tears in their eyes, what had happened. I acted as coolly as I could, kissed Karl, and said to him:

"Dear Karl, you have accepted the punishment of your own free will, and you wanted to take it honestly. For that reason, and for the sake of our intended walk and the request of our friends, I want you to consider it finished. Go on eating your cake and drinking your milk! You have fulfilled the law. I free you from everything."

Now Karl gratefully and gladly partook of the offered food. The E.'s could not understand how it was possible for a child of six years to have such self-control as to deny himself a favorite dish, under the above-mentioned circumstances and with his good appetite.

They did not know sufficiently the high power of a pure piety and the resulting morality, for with it much more can be done, without it but little.

A second principle was the development and strengthening of his body and, as much as possible, its separate powers. Here also naturally belong the sharpening and strengthening of the senses.

A third principle was, from the very beginning, the highest development of his mental powers, in all their several capacities—reason, acute perception, wit, memory, fancy, and so forth. I have already said something of this, but I will now discuss it at greater length.

Here belongs the acquisition of a literary language, with correct thinking, questioning, answering, retorting, etc., which so pleasantly surprised people. It was for this reason that his company was enjoyed even before he had learned the least thing about the languages or sciences. How many splendid pleasures have thus been granted to Karl, and how much he has heard, seen, and learned by it!

The most cultured men of the regions where I happened to sojourn or to visit, gladly showed or had shown to the child anything that would cause him pleasure, and thus his childhood, on account of the very goodness of his heart, passed under the noblest enjoyments and constant instruction.

It was in his sixth year that his linguistic instruction began, and from his clear conviction that he needed it for his welfare, from the employment of a proper and simple method, as well as from a cautiously chosen sequence of the same, his acquisition of foreign languages became a not very difficult struggle with single words and their forms. In fact, his exercises in the reading of foreign languages soon grew to be for him what the exercises in reading German had been—a most agreeable entertainment, a pleasant pastime, during which it did not even occur to him that he was learning uncommonly much.

The instruction in the sciences had long been prepared, by discussions, visits to a thousand memorable things, by journeys, by stories from ancient and modern history, and by his own reading in all the languages known to him.

He was ever anxious to know more, and eagerly asked for what has to be imparted to other children with the greatest difficulty. He studied ancient and modern geography, natural history in all its branches, mathematics, physics, and chemistry, and he studied them so thoroughly that he received his degree of Doctor of Philosophy before he was fourteen, after having previously obtained very flattering certificates. A year later he became a member of the Society of Natural Sciences in the Wetterau. He was then able to live in the beautiful region of the Rhine, and to study jurisprudence with its ancillary sciences so thoroughly that when he was but sixteen he was honorably advanced to the degree of Doctor of Laws. Then he traveled a great deal, lived for a longer time in Berlin, had a mass of pleasant and some very unpleasant experiences, was treated by many noble men with love, by a few mean ones with malice, received from his king the high favor of a two years' scientific journey, and could use the interim to prepare himself theoretically and practically for that honorable and useful commission.

CHAPTER XI

Should Children be Left to Themselves up to their Seventh or Eighth Year?

It is a very natural question, "At what period should we begin to instruct our children?" It has become fashionable to answer, with Rousseau, "From the seventh or eighth year." To all those who answer thus, I have nothing to say but this: "Watch the children who have so long remained without instruction or even without an education, and see what has become of them. You will generally find that they have turned out to be self-willed, violent, even ignorant creatures, slaves to their desires and vices. If you wish to have such children, good and well,—do as those parents have done!"

I once spoke to a man who claimed to know all about education and who expressed himself contemptuously about my son who had at such an early age been trained to external and internal good manners.

"No," said he, "that shall not happen with my son. He is to enjoy his childhood. Up to his eighth year he is to do as he pleases, being left only to his nurse and to his mother." [1]

"Then you will have little to educate in him later," I quickly retorted.

The outcome showed that I was right. Though the boy possessed excellent mental capacities, he turned out to be nothing but an ordinary man with many faults. Had he been simple-minded, his father, through his own fault, would have made a fool of him.

It may be objected that there are great men who must have traveled that same path. Indeed, there are, but they are rare. Only because they discovered themselves and attracted the attention of others they and their early lives became known, and the foolish conclusion was drawn that that was the right way. But one will always, or at least most frequently, find in them dark sides as well as bright ones, for the early acquired and deeply rooted faults are very hard to get rid of. It would be an easy matter for me to find some humiliating defect in any great man who has been

[1] This mother lived entirely for society, so the child was left in the care of servants.

brought up in that way; but I refrain from doing so, because it would be wrong, in the manner of evil-minded persons, to try to drag great men into the dust.

He who advocates that method of education as the best, overlooks the fact that a man with very great capacities,—a real genius—will always succeed and become something great, but that all those who have only mediocre or humble capacities will be ruined, and there are infinitely more of these than of geniuses. One forgets to observe how noble, sublime, and useful such a genius might have become, if he had been properly guided and educated from the start.

The same man who, on account of the bad sides in his character, had risen to eighty degrees, by careful guidance and beneficently molded circumstances, might have risen to a hundred—that is, to the highest degree of possible human perfection, and that, too, on the good side of him.

If a child is left to himself or to the servants, he naturally associates with other children in the street. At first only with those of neighbors, then with their friends and acquaintances, and finally with all children, for man is a social being, and children as a rule prefer children's society. Then they like to play, and play in the open rightly pleases them most, because God has blessed the air with so many refreshing, strengthening, exhilarating elements. Therefore the child feels happiest in the open, especially if he can there play with other children.

Had I to choose, I would myself, in spite of the great dangers connected with being in the street, prefer it to the constant staying in the room. I am not talking of Berlin rooms. These, as a rule are high, airy, bright, pleasant, large, and, if the parents do right, may act as small play halls for the children. No, I am talking of rooms in small towns or in the country, where the whole family is usually stuffed together in a small, low, narrow, damp basement, filled with all kinds of utensils.

Here the children waste away, their power of digestion is diminished, their blood creeps along, instead of leaping, their cheeks grow pale, their eyes become dimmed, and the fire of their spirits slowly goes out. Stomach, head, and teeth begin to ache, there follow indisposition and ennui, and, in their wake, contrariness, stubbornness, a spirit of opposition, or even servility, dullness, prejudice, and short-sightedness. The healthy street urchin may some day do something right. Often he takes his own peculiar course and breaks new paths, whereas such a dwarfed little man as the room-dweller is generally good for nothing but a house-savant. In that vocation he finds the familiar surroundings and remains bodily and spiritually in his element.

Yet I do not overlook the great dangers that await the boy amidst his playmates in the street. How could I overlook them? I have myself observed and anxiously watched them. I will not speak here of the secret temptations for masturbation, the most terrible of juvenile vices, of the incitements for disobeying the parents and showing them disrespect, of deception and even thieving, and so forth. They occur, indeed, only too often, and their consequences are appalling. But I wish to speak only of that which takes place openly, during the playing in the street.

In some places, among others at G., where the large stone slabs near the houses favor many children's games, one constantly sees children gambling for money. They are often so poor that one would feel like giving them alms, and yet they play for pennies and threepence, and win from or lose dimes to children whose parents are rich. Many a time I have called out to them, "Youthful gamblers, old deceivers or beggars!" If it has done good only once! Besides, I have hardly ever walked through the town without seeing two or three in a fight. This at first begins with some little dissension, which passes over to scolding and cursing, and ends in fighting, in kicking, throwing stones, etc. "Fury changes everything into weapons," says Virgil.

With mortal fear I have watched such fights, and have done all in my power to stop them. But I have at last become more indifferent, for I thought of myself as of one with weak nerves who is worried at the very thought that somebody might just then be struggling in death agony. He then has not a calm moment in his life, for he must always say to himself, "Now somebody is again struggling in death agony." Just the same happens to a philanthropist during a fight. He must at last become indifferent to it, or he will neglect his business in his eternal attempts to make peace.

In some places there has grown up the custom of throwing sand. It begins in jest and ends in the most terrible earnest, for, if one happens to turn around just as the other is throwing, he gets the sand, with the splinters and pebbles, which the other has hurriedly picked up, straight into his eyes. One is lucky if it only causes pain, and the eye does not suffer from it. As a rule, it leads to the heaviest fighting.

In other places snowballing is indulged in in the winter. There would be no objection to it, were it only kept within bounds. Throwing soft snowballs is a merry jest, productive of agility, quickness, attention, and sturdiness. But the balls grow harder and harder. Many boys knead them for a long time with their hands, so as to make them small and moist, then let them lie in rows and get frozen, and finally take them secretly to the place where they expect to find their acquaintances. Such a snowball causes pain in the back or the chest, but what if it strikes the face or an eye? And the boy who has brought it along is sure to throw it with all his might and at as close a range as he can get.

More than once have I seen the blood flow freely on such an occasion, or the nose or eye injured for life.

How often have I been a witness when children in a sham battle have accidentally caused bad injuries or have been incited to violent fights from which such injuries resulted. I still think with horror of a pupil,—I will call him Mueller,—who played at H., near the parade grounds, close to the high school, with his companions. The grounds are surrounded by a wall, and trees and buildings are not far off. Mueller for a long time ran deftly among these objects without hurting himself. I was afraid for him, but he ran too fast and was pursued too closely, and I was too far away to stop him with my voice.

Now his pursuers were upon him. He wanted to get away from them by running into the school building. One side of the door was open, the other was closed, being barred at the top and bottom. Mueller ran as fast as he could, and turned his head in order to get in through the open side. But he was too close and so ran with all his might against the projecting bar which was studded with nails. At the same moment the blood ran in streams down his face, and he fell to the ground with a cry of anguish.

I have often tried to find out why this boy had his hand or foot maimed, why that boy was crippled, a third one had disfiguring tumors or cuts in his face, a fourth one had a growth on his eye, a fifth was, perhaps, bereft of an eye, and I have learned that all this was caused in the street. The children had naturally concealed the occurrence from their parents, and thus had prevented the timely aid of a surgeon, of whom, through their parents' fault, they are nearly always in fear.

It will be noticed that I know all the mischief, and that I do not take it lightly, but I must repeat my conviction: If I should have to choose, I would, in spite of the above-mentioned great dangers, which come from being in the street, prefer it to the eternal staying in the house. All those who are lucky enough to survive are far better off than the effeminate house-dolls who are terrified at the very sight of a soft snowball, and whom a drizzle or a cool wind puts on the sick-bed.

I say, then, Woe to the father or educator who is so foolish as to say: "My son shall do up to his eighth year as he pleases, for up to that time he shall be left in charge of his nurse and his mother (a society woman)."

From all that it follows that we must begin very early to educate our children, and not only this but we ought to endeavor to bring into the world children as little handicapped as possible by defects transmitted by us. Let us pay attention to our bodies, our intellects, our wills (both on the part of the father and the mother); let us ennoble the first two and control the latter, even at a time when our children have not yet been procreated. A simple, moderate, sparing, satisfied, happy life, with much exercise in the open air, frequent use of pure water, is, as a rule, the best means for getting children whose bodies will be entirely sound, and whose capacities of heart and intellect are equally desirable. A man should train himself as much as possible, and should choose for himself a healthy, mentally well-developed, and well-intentioned wife, and then the children will be healthy, mentally strong, and well-intentioned.

Here I hear a mass of objections.

One says, "In my situation I must marry for money." Another says, "Without the distinguished relatives of my wife I should never have reached the security which I am enjoying." A third, "My wife danced so well that I was charmed by her." A fourth, "My wife charmed me by her clever and witty conversation." A fifth says, "I loved her, and I was looking for a wife for myself, not a mother for my children," etc.

I answer, "Gentlemen, you may all be right in your way! But if the question is about expecting to have fine children, then you are all wrong."

After everything possible has been done for one's children before their procreation, one should double the precautions during the mother's pregnancy. Both parents must cooperate in this.

Moderation and simplicity in food, drink, and the enjoyment of corporal love, much exercise in the open, pure drinking water, the most scrupulous bodily cleanliness, strict execution of duties, contentment, joyfulness, and faith in God.

Those are the surest means which the mother can use, in order to provide the germinating child with the most wholesome and useful nourishment. If the father sweetens her life by thinking, feeling, and acting in the same way, both may be assured that the Deity will, as a rule, give them a healthy child that is, at the very least, provided with average capacities of body and mind. Nothing more is required.

CHAPTER XII

What we did to Guard Karl against Flattery, or, at Least, to Weaken its Venom

Karl was but sparingly praised by us, some such expression as, "All right, my son!" or "Well done, my boy!" or "You may be right!" or "Yes, that is right!" being all I used to express my approbation. Some other stimuli were employed, for example, small rewards, with which, however, charitable purposes were invisibly connected; the noting down of his conduct in a book which Konsistorialrath Dr. Funk of Magdeburg had presented to him; a calm yet pleasant recital of what he had accomplished to his mother or one of the more intimate friends of the family. But I every time said rather less than more. The person listening to the account would then reply, "Well, that pleases me, Karl! I like you that way!" or something of the kind.

Karl had to have done something extraordinary for his age, before he was patted or kissed. That I gladly did, every time he said or did something morally good. A fondling, a kiss from me, was therefore highly appreciated by him. But nothing had such an effect with him as the assurance I gave him especially at a noteworthy moment of his life, that he now, no doubt, was standing higher than ever in the eyes of God, of other spiritual beings, and of the best of men, and that for some time he had profitably and successfully prepared himself to do something really good on earth and later to be employed by the Deity for higher and more profitable purposes.

Then his childishly pious eye would smile to us, as we may imagine the beatitude of an angel who after a noble adventure in the great kingdom of God returns to the Highest. Usually Karl, after such a conversation, evinced still more docility, more industry, more goodness of heart than heretofore. There was therefore no need of greater praise, much less of flattery. But most people who lived outside our circle did not appreciate this, and many did not want to comprehend it.

If, for example, it was noticed that, in spite of my enthusiasm, I praised my son with cool consideration, trying to lessen the value of what he had said or done, and actually succeeding in lessening it—they attributed to me, instead of God-fearing purposes, such traits as harshness, stubbornness, pride, injustice, arbitrariness, and even envy toward my own child, because they, the mean ones, could not rise to the higher purposes. If, again, I told the truth about him in his absence, such a fatherly feeling was denominated vanity or pride.

Such wry judgments were often uttered in Karl's presence, and for ten or twelve years they have tried hard, by sarcasms and expressions of pity, and by actual incitement during my absence to cause a rupture between me and my wife. If I had not been absolutely just, and at the same time reasonable and kind, those wretches would have actually succeeded in it.

Those who were somewhat better said with wise mien whenever, in their opinion, I did not praise enough, or sent Karl away, as soon as I surmised that the cloud of praise would be discharged in the boy's presence, "Oh, but that is not at all right of you! He has deserved it, and merited praise encourages one!"

It made no difference how much I implored them to be careful, they knew better, at least they thought they knew better, and they only broke forth more loudly in Karl's presence.

It did not take me long to perceive the weakness or meanness of many of my friends and neighbors. I was therefore careful to make my arrangements accordingly. I withdrew completely from some, to a great extent from others. And as often as, against my expectation, it became necessary for the good of my child, I had no hesitation to speak clearly and earnestly about the dangers of fulsome praise. Karl understood me in such cases completely, but those silly wiseacres naturally became only more wily toward me.

In connection with sugar, cake, coffee, beer, wine, and other dainties the same thing took place. But my close friends, partly better, partly more educated men, were exceedingly useful to me in this matter. They understood what I wanted, and magnanimously offered a helping hand. I needed only to give them a hint, and they worked into my hands.

If my wife or I was dissatisfied with Karl, they never defended him, but, on the contrary, treated him with some coolness. If we gave a friendly utterance about him, he was heartily fondled by them, but they did not overflow with praise.

As long as he was very small and had learned little or nothing, we accomplished our aim by means of our unfailing device, the recital of short, purposely invented, stories with a moral.

But when he could recite with expression, when, to the astonishment of many men, he could do mental calculations, when he could read rapidly and very well, and even began to understand French, I had to have recourse to other means as well.

The highest from the beginning and for all time remained God and His visible counterpart among men, Jesus.

In conversations about God I frequently showed him how immeasurably deep we stood below Him and below those many millions of spiritual beings whom we call by the name of angels: I showed him that we owed Him ourselves, all our bodily and mental powers, our fortunes, our education, even the incitements to do good. On such convictions it is, indeed, easy to found humility of spirit and modesty in a still childishly pure mind.

In the person of Jesus we showed him how infinitely much a man, even of the highest type, may by modesty and humility gain of wisdom, mental power, magnanimity, firmness, kindness of heart, justice, fair-mindedness, faith in God, submission to His will, obedience to His commands, patience, and denial of oneself.

Thus there arose in his heart the highest reverence for God, the strongest, holiest love for Jesus, and the eager desire to become like Him. My wife Louise or I had only to mention an incident in the life of Jesus, which in some way cast a light on one of His virtues, for Karl to understand us at once, and to try in a touching manner to apply it himself. He naturally found himself always far below the Divinity, consequently he was by every comparison, even without any other admixture, urgently led on toward modesty.

Then we told him a great deal about eminent men. If they excelled in intellect, ability, talents, and so forth, we accentuated these so clearly and so objectively that the humiliating conviction of having to climb an immeasurable height up to them must have forced itself upon him, though we laid less stress upon that. But what information we gave him about noble-minded, virtuous men, their God-pleasing, pious, humanely friendly actions, was imparted,— as indeed it could not, from the state of our feelings, be imparted otherwise,—with ardor, with holy joy, sometimes even with tears. Thus his heart was touched and moved, and the desire to act similarly was aroused in him.

Whenever small occasions offered themselves, he of his own accord acted as we had wished; if he did not, we reminded him of the story and then we were certain not to miss our aim.

He knew by heart nearly all the poems from the golden period of German poetry, which inculcated noble actions, sacrifices for others, love of man, goodness of heart, magnanimity, friendship, and so forth. He learned them readily and easily, and made their contents completely his own.

The "Lied vom Braven Mann," "Frau Magdalis," "Zu Dionys dem Tyrannen Schlich," "Rudolph von Habsburg," etc., were his favorite poems, and he knew them all by heart, long though they are.

Now I ask any sensible man and experienced educator: Could a boy with all that become proud, vain, and immodest?

Not easily! And of a child that is not often flattered I would say, Not at all!

This venom (flattery) was, however, given him more and more as time went on. It was given to him in many shapes, and so I had to think of all kinds of antidotes.

We once went to the city of Halle, and I guessed in advance that in the company with whom we were to dine, and in the homes where we were to visit, Karl, as usual, would be showered with praise.

So after we had set out for Halle I began with Louise, who understood me at once, an apparently general conversation about compliments, laudations, and flattery. We talked as though we did not have Karl in mind, but in reality kept a close watch on him. Now and then I threw in a few words, which I expected to affect him more strongly, and which he would understand as referring to him.

He comprehended, as showed itself soon afterward, that some men, from a certain softness of spirit which is wrongly called kindness of heart, like to tell pleasant things to another; that evil men frequently do so in order to gain advantages for themselves; that ignorant people, without being evil, readily do the same thing because they have an exaggerated idea of what they have not learned themselves; and that, finally, there are men who try to use flattery, because they consider it a sign of refinement not to say anything unpleasant to their acquaintances, or, rather, to tell them pleasant things, even if they are not true.

True praise, I added, is not wordy. It finds its expression rather in a tender glance, a soft pressure of the hand, a few sincerely pronounced syllables, at times even in a mere stroking of the cheek, or in a kiss, but above all else in love and kindness, or in acceptable actions for the good of those who have earned the praise.

As Pastor J. lately did with me, I continued, and told a story of how a friend of mine, instead of making me compliments for some mental labor, or flattering me, took particular pains to make such remarks as would help me to improve that work.

With such conversation we approached the city. I became jocose and said:

"You will notice at the very gate that people for a mere trifle make compliments, that is, say something with which they connect no idea at all, or the very opposite idea. Since I am in the habit of giving the gatekeeper a few cents, he will come leaping out merrily and will tell me that he is my humble servant, will inquire about my health, and will assure me that he is extremely happy to hear of my well-being; he will ask what my orders are, and will add that he is convinced that I have nothing dutiable about me." (I knew the man's ways of talking by rote.) "He would be considerably surprised," I added, "if to his 'humble servant' I should say, 'Please, take off my boots and shine them for me, for they have become dirty on the road,' or if I asked him to swear to his assertion that he was extremely happy to hear of my well-being; or if to his question, 'What are your orders?' I should answer, 'Go at once to Professor W. and announce our arrival!' or if his superior would take him to task, 'How is it that you are convinced that the pastor has nothing dutiable about him?'

"Yet that man speaks German," I went on, "and good German at that, so he knows what his utterances are. You see, one would be very much deceived, if one paid attention to such words. What is still stranger, is that some people feel that the parents are too sensible and too earnest to have any compliments made to them, so they think they can make them the compliments through their children.

"As is well known, most parents love in their children not only the higher being that God has enclosed in a body and has entrusted them with, but also, animal-like, their young ones. Thus a man like G. imagines that Witte will not be so insensible as to remain indifferent toward the praise which he bestows on Karl. Karl need only keep from doing something unseemly, to be extolled with swollen cheeks, so that I am ashamed and afraid for Karl. For what can the poor boy answer to such untruths? He must remain perplexed. That is why I like R. and W. They praise truly and sensibly. G. gains his end with hundreds of parents, but the children are spoiled by it, for they become conceited and believe they know all.

"It is strangest of all," I continued, "when parents want to hear their children praised, while an honest man cannot make up his mind to please them by doing so. It may be that he will pay the tribute of customary politeness, if the children give half an occasion for it. But the honest man will not be induced to do more than that.

"Meanwhile these people try their uttermost to get at him, to melt the ice of insensibility. If the honest man has children of his own, they expect to have an easy success, if they will praise them unduly. 'He will certainly be polite enough to give something in return!' they say, and so they lavish praises, until one is nauseated and has to remonstrate. That stops the praises, but immediately afterward they say, 'Witte is an uncouth man! I praised his Karl so much, but it did not do any good. I hoped he would say a word about my Fritz or Dorothy, but no! Does he imagine he can educate all children? There is not much to it anyway! His Karl lacks a lot of things which he is much in need of.

"They are right there, my boy. Do you not think so?"

Karl assented to it with his whole soul, mentioned some things which he needed, and named men who had praised him, partly without any merit of his, partly away above his deserts.

"I have seen the case," I or Louise added, "when two fathers or mothers carried on a regular auction sale. One would outbid the other in praises, until the conviction was forced upon a person that the respective children were half angels, when they were nothing of the sort. For had they been, their parents would not have taken these useless, even harmful, pains."

Now we were at the gate. We had no sooner stopped, than the gatekeeper, who knew the coachman, carriage, and horses well, rushed out and started turning the wheel of compliments with almost the very words which I had predicted. As none of us could help smiling, I gave the conversation a joking turn by saying, "We have nothing about us, unless we ourselves are dutiable. O yes, here I have," pointing to Karl, "a little gosling!

So have him appraised! Meanwhile, here is the money!" I pressed a little something into his hand. We proceeded to the city, and I said earnestly, "So all that has cost only two dimes!"

The consequences of that conversation were obviously good, but I must make a remark here.

One must not imagine that such a conversation with Karl or in his presence would have had the desired result in itself. I am, on the contrary, convinced that without a previous long, careful education of mind and heart; without repeated and continuous paternal efforts; without the aid of our excellent friends; without deep-seated moral and pious motives, all that attempt would not have succeeded in penetrating the hardened shell, and would have produced weak, effaceable impressions upon the intellect and the heart. It is about the same as with a wagon whose freight is calculated for three horses. If only one were hitched, it would work itself to death without moving the wagon an inch. To make it move, and move with ease, all three horses must be employed. Then it is sure to travel well.

Since many people are convinced that Karl has always been perfect; that he could not perceive any faults or mistakes in himself; that he must have become conscious of being far in advance of other children; and that that must have driven him to pride and vanity, I shall remind them of what has been mentioned before. We frequently referred in his presence to what he would have turned out to be, if he had grown up without careful training and instruction, and what many a child would have developed into, if he had been brought to our house at his birth, and we had accepted and educated him as our own child. We also explained to Karl how much more advanced in every respect he would be, if he had always been attentive and industrious. But he knew only too well, how often he had failed in one respect or other. His memory and his "Book of Conduct" told him that.

If, during such a talk, I should happen to see a shepherd boy, who had to pasture the cattle, instead of being at school—and I took care to arrange our walk in such a way as to see him—I would say, with deeply felt pity, "The poor boy! He should now be in school learning something, but he must pasture cattle in order to earn a living, for his father has nine children and is too poor to be able to feed him, if he does not take the place of a hired hand. You know, my son, how cleverly this boy talks! What could not have been made of him, if he had been properly brought up!" Then I spoke to the shepherd boy, and directed his attention to how much he was losing by not going more frequently to school, and urged upon him to attend school more regularly in winter.

That never missed its aim. Karl's heart was sincerely moved to pity, and his intellect saw clearly that he owed the little he was and knew, not to himself, but to his parents.

How would it have been possible to save him from the venom of flattery without such precautionary measures? I dare say, but few children grow up with as much flattery as has been showered upon him, yet, thank Heaven, it has caused him no harm, as all know who are more closely acquainted with him.

"He must be proud," said the most sensible and excellent Konsistorialrath Dr. Senf, of Halle, before he knew him. "He must be!" he said again and again, "for with his advantages it is against human nature not to be proud!" I kept repeating, "No, he is not!" "He must be," he finally said, with emphasis, "or he is a supernatural being." I kept silent, for to that no answer could be given. "You shall see him," I retorted after a while.

I brought the boy to him soon afterward. He immediately fondled him with much tenderness, had a long talk with him, spoke ever in a more fatherly and intimate way to him, and finally turned to me and said, "No, he is not proud! God knows how you have managed it!" After I had sent Karl out, I gave Dr. Senf an account of the above-mentioned method. He nodded friendly assent from time to time, and finished by saying:

"Yes, it is possible to do so in that manner! I now believe myself that he is not proud and will never become proud. For if, with these convictions, he attains still greater reasoning power, he will become what is called wise. And a truly reasoning, wise man cannot be proud."

I pass for the present over those innumerable perplexities which were caused to me by wealthy and distinguished people of both sexes, by regents, their wives, their children, their entourage; and will mention but one occurrence, at Goettingen, because it best illustrates my anxiety and my way of acting under such conditions.

A director of schools at N., named H., was visiting his relatives at Goettingen. He had heard and read a great deal about Karl, and he had learned still more, after inquiries at Goettingen, especially from his relatives who were more closely acquainted with us. He therefore requested them to invite us to their home when he was with them, and to arrange it in such a way that he could examine Karl. They readily promised to do this, as they knew I should have no objections.

We accepted the invitation and granted the request about the examination. H. in person had repeated the latter to me, adding that he would gladly examine my son in the languages and the various sciences, but preferably in mathematics, because that was his favorite subject. I granted him everything, making, as with everybody else, the one condition that he would not praise the boy, or would praise him only moderately, if he should be satisfied with his knowledge.

"You may love him," I added, half in jest,

"as much as you wish, but you must not praise him! But you are yourself a father and educator. My request is therefore not necessary with you, and I beg your pardon for it."

Karl, whom we had purposely sent out, came in. H. was soon occupied with him, and his talk with him quickly passed into a formal examination.

As I shall have to speak later in regard to such tests of his knowledge, I shall merely remark that H. was perfectly satisfied with him, that he fondled Karl in a fatherly way, but judiciously avoided nearly all praise. I kept a watch upon him, and so was fairly easy in mind. Finally he passed over to mathematics and proposed to Karl several problems in geometry, etc. Karl answered the questions with ease, and frequently in more than one way. He also put himself at H.'s standpoint, accepted his methods of proof, and, without being at all familiar with it, applied it to H.'s full satisfaction.

Here a few expressions of praise escaped him that I thought were too strong. I, therefore, looked more sharply at him, and he understood me and kept silent.

But the examiner and the examinee entered

the subject more deeply, and as they grew to consider each other as friends who loved and discussed the same science, they soon lost themselves in higher mathematics, even in such branches as were not entirely familiar to H.

"Oh, you know more of this than I!" escaped his lips, in his pleased surprise. I was frightened, but I managed to sound a warning note.

"My son attended the mathematical lectures last half-year," I said, "and so he has not forgotten it yet."

H. understood me, and held himself in. After a while he said to Karl:

"Now I will close by laying before you a proposition over which the great Euler brooded in vain for three days. I presume that you have not heard of it."

I was beginning to feel anxious, in case Karl should actually solve it, but did not dare to let this be noticed, because H., who did not know me intimately, might have considered it as a sign of fatherly pride. And if I should have interrupted the conversation—which I was inclined to do—he might have thought that I was afraid Karl could not solve it, and that I, from pride, was ashamed because he could not. H. then went on to propound the problem.

"A peasant," said he, "had a field of this shape:

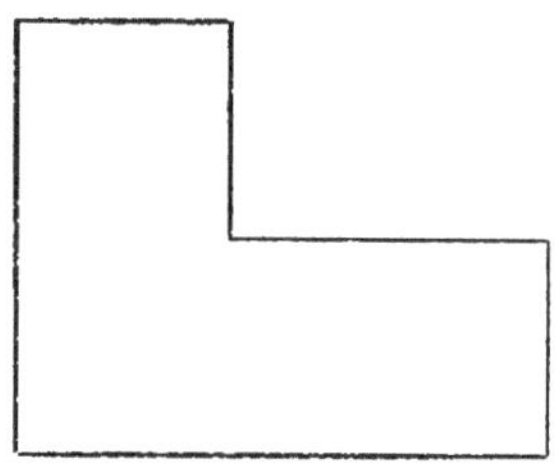

"When he was near death, he called his three sons and directed them so to divide the field that each should obtain an equal share, each of these to be similar to the whole field.

"Have you had this proposition, or have you read about it?" he asked Karl once more, with emphasis.

Karl answered "No!" and I testified to it, because I had always shared his mathematical instruction with him.

Then we gave him time for reflection, and H., talking with me in the back of the room, declared that it would certainly be impossible for him to solve the problem. "I proposed it to him only to show him that he did not know everything yet."

He had hardly said more than that, when Karl called out:

"I have it!"

"That is impossible!" H. exclaimed, in perplexity.

"See for yourself!" Karl said, as he drew the lines which he had only sketched before. "These three fields are equal to each other and similar to the whole field."

"You must have known the proposition!" H. exclaimed, with violence and bitter contempt.

Karl felt deeply ashamed, and repeated with tears in his eyes, "No!"

I could not remain silent. I gave him the most solemn assurances that Karl had not heard of it before, and especially that Karl would not be so contemptible as to deny anything of the sort, or to stick to a lie impudently.

"Then he must be greater than the great Euler himself!" H. answered, still in doubt, and staring at Karl.

I anxiously called out from the back of the room, where I stood, "Not at all! For you, as an experienced man, must know," I said, pinching his hand, and then laughing, "that even blind pigeons sometimes find peas."

H. understood me, and replied, distractedly, "Of course, indeed!" and immediately turning to me, he said in a whisper, "Only in this way have you been able so to educate a son as to leave him exceedingly modest with such knowledge."

But Karl had in the meanwhile gotten up a merry conversation with his neighbor on an entirely different subject, and that, justly, pleased H. most of all.

CHAPTER XIII

KARL'S TOYS AND THE FIRST STEPS IN HIS MENTAL EDUCATION

I AM convinced that we cannot begin too early to play with a child, and that we may turn nearly all objects of life into toys of great educational value, if we only go about it in the right way.

Playing with the little child should be an easy, pleasing occupation, with which to awaken, guide, and strengthen his dormant powers. One should begin with the coarsest, most sensuous objects, for the finer ones would as yet be lost on the child.

For example, we held our fingers close to Karl's eyes, and moved them, now singly, now several at a time. He soon noticed them, and grabbed at them, but in the beginning usually missed them. We did not mind that, but brought our hand nearer to his, or his nearer to ours. He seized it, happy to have succeeded, and drew a finger into his mouth and sucked it. Then we pronounced the word "finger" slowly, distinctly, and repeatedly, so that the unreasoning being might have the time to hear it clearly and to conceive it. After a few minutes we withdrew our finger from his mouth, and held it once more before his eyes, first one, saying, "One finger," then two, in the same way saying, "Two fingers," and so forth.

If he grabbed the thumb, we should have said, as above, "Thumb." At first, however, we avoided his getting hold of it, in order not to confuse the still indescribable short-sightedness of his intellect. When he actually knew the fingers, we gave him the thumb, pronouncing the word at the same time. We slowly differentiated the pointer, the middle finger, the little finger. In every case the road was properly prepared, and the words were enunciated loudly, clearly, slowly, and repeatedly.

Later on we put the fingers to some use before his eyes, from mere moving to the raising of his hand or an object, and all the time did and spoke as above.

For his hearing we made use perhaps of two smooth keys which we struck together before Karl's eyes and ears alternately, enunciating the word "Key." If he at last seized it, he carried it to his mouth, and we by degrees proceeded farther, holding more keys before him and speaking, as mentioned above.

It will be easily observed that with prudence and care one may thus turn any object into a toy, and I am convinced that one does much better to follow this course than to buy a mass of toys for the child and leave him to an arbitrary use of them, without any prudent guidance. The unreasoning little people may only hurt themselves with them, and learn nothing; they pass their time half senselessly, become tired, irritable, stubborn, and throw their toys away, or pound at them; in short, they become accustomed to destructiveness, as one, alas, finds only too often.

This habit of destruction is so bad, that I regretfully reflect upon the fact that it clings to man for a long time, frequently misguides him, and makes it hard for him to rid himself of it. Observant parents will understand me, for they must have noticed what a deleterious influence the destruction habit has on the intellectual conceptions, as well as on the sentiments of children.

The child vents his displeasure,—itself usually a result of ennui,—on his toys; later on, he vents it on what he can reach; at last also on his animal and human surroundings. Anybody can see what sad consequences this must have.

I should become too prolix if I were to mention and explain our educational methods in detail. A few hints are all that is needed. Some I have already given, and I will give a few more now.

As soon as Karl had reached a certain degree of perception, we proceeded to another stage in the enlargement of his understanding. After a while, for example, we brought him a twig, and said, "A twig," then we brought a leaf from it, and holding it before his eyes, we said "A leaf." We alternated twig and leaf several times, giving the little fellow time to collect his senses, and every time said loudly, clearly, and slowly, "A twig, a leaf." By degrees we plucked a few more leaves from the twig, saying, "One more leaf, one more leaf." Then we put two leaves before him, saying, "See, Karl! Two leaves!" then "Three leaves!" etc.

At other times we pointed to the twig,

which still had a few leaves upon it, saying, with clear enunciation and much emphasis, "One leaf, two leaf," and quickly correcting ourselves, "Two leaves," at last, with the expression of surprise, "Many leaves!"

When the twig was slowly bared of all leaves, we switched it in the air, and said, "A switch!"

"See, Karl! Now it is a switch! Now the leaves are all gone," pointing to them, "they are pulled off, and now it is not a twig, now it is a switch!"

After a while again we would say, "I cut the twig from a tree. Come, and I will show you where I cut it off!" Then we took him in our arms, or by his hand, and led him to the tree, from which we had cut the twig, so low down that he could easily observe it. We fitted on the twig, and later the switch, and said, slowly, clearly, and distinctly, "Do you see? Here I cut it from the tree," pointing meanwhile to the whole tree. "This is the way it stuck to the tree before."

Then I would, perhaps, say, "Shall I cut off another twig?"

He was sure to answer, "Yes!"

Now, purposely of course, I would look

in vain for a knife in all my pockets, repeatedly saying, "I have no knife about me, and without a knife I cannot cut the twig from the tree." After a few moments: "Wait, my child! I will fetch a knife!"

After I had fetched it, I said, pointing to it, "Here I have a knife! Now I can cut a twig with it from the tree."

I did so, significantly raised the twig, and said: "Now, the twig is cut off the tree!" and after a while, "See, Karl," fitting the twig once more to the tree, "here the twig was attached to the tree." Then, holding it up, together with the one cut off before, "Now we have two twigs!"

At first we used to say, "Now we have one twig, and one twig more," pointing all the time to a twig, "so now we have two twigs."

Only later we directed his attention to the various sizes of trees. We would, for example, first point to a dwarfed tree, saying, "This tree is small!" then to a young tree with a tall trunk, saying, "This tree is taller," finally to an old, tall tree, saying, "This tree is very tall." Everything was enunciated with the proper intonation and with the appropriate expression and motion of the hands Thus we taught him as play, entertainment, and pastime, that certain trees (this one here, that one there) bore beautiful blossoms and good-tasting fruits while other trees did not.

If, by chance, it happened to be an oak, I would say, as though wishing to correct an error:

"That is an oak! I have not told you right, for the oaks bear also fruit, only we, men, cannot eat it. Pigs like it very much. You shall see for yourself!"

If acorns could be found, we picked up a few, giving them to Karl to take along and throw to our pig. If it was before acorn time, I would hunt for them for a while, then act as though I were deep in thought, and finally say:

"Oh, yes, I happen to think, there are no ripe acorns now. Just look up there in the tree! There are acorns there! But they are still very small. In a few weeks they will be larger. Perhaps a few of them will then fall down. We will pick them up then and take them with us."

In a similar manner we proceeded with a thousand objects all about us; for example, with a rose.

We would break off a branch with several leaves, a few buds, a half-opened and a fully-opened rose, and would lay the whole before him with the words, "Here you have a twig off a rose-bush!" Then we took everything up in succession: twig, leaves, stems, thorns (larger, smaller, straight, crooked), hairs, calyx, flower, colored leaves, outer, inner, large, small, smooth, curly, curved, folded, white, pink, red; the anthers, stamens, pollen, the closed bud (which we finally opened up), the half-opened, etc. Among other things, toward the end, we referred to the smell, which was at once observed and compared with that of other flowers and plants.

It will be noticed that the most ordinary surroundings furnish a field for play and instruction, which is more than large and rich enough to give the child a sufficient choice of mental food for the first five or six years of his life.

I must remark here that whoever learns in this manner to hear, see, feel, smell, taste, will certainly learn it all in the proper way, gaining therewith so much mental power that also his spiritual hearing, seeing, and feeling, as well as careful observation and taste will be ennobled by it in a startling manner.

The above-mentioned method was of importance, too, in regard to the child's morality. If Karl was dissatisfied or crying, because he could not have his way, we only had to say, "Just see how queer this is!" showing him something that was new to him, in order to turn his attention away upon it. He forgot his ill temper, and was once more the good, merry child. He never went so far as to bawl and bellow.

I hardly ever bought toys, in the ordinary sense of the word. This expense I was spared, because everything was a plaything to him.

The best opportunity was furnished by a fairly large space in front of my house, which I had covered two feet deep with clear pebbles, and faced in with flowers, blooming shrubs, and trees. This spot was always dry, even after days of rain. After an hour's cessation, the rain-water disappeared between the pebbles, and the place was again quite dry and healthy.

Here and in the garden, when it was not damp, Karl lived and worked amid fair Nature. At first his attention was directed to all the details around him. Later on he observed them himself, and showed them to us, partly with the desire of instructing us, and partly in order to elicit instruction from us.

Whenever I, on account of other business, was not able to be with him, my wife was near by. Whenever she had to attend to some housework or to the garden, he stood, sat, or walked with her, and both discussed what had been done, what was being done, or what still had to be done.

And he not only had the permission openly to tell us his opinion pro and con,—of course, with due modesty,—but we urged him on to do so. We sometimes would purposely make small mistakes or overlook something, and merrily berated him, if he did not notice our faults.

Every little work gave us chances for this, the cutting of the asparagus, picking of roses or fruit, and so forth. If we had found some good reason for not doing a certain thing, and he reminded us of it, as of something we might have forgotten or overlooked, we again made good-natured fun of him, saying, "O you foolish boy! Do you not understand that I did not do it for such and such a reason?"

Such discussions sufficiently guarded him against the presumption,—for which occasions often presented themselves,—of knowing better than we.

One of his earliest games was with sand. I bought him for the purpose a little table and chair, when he was about two years old. I still have them, and they will remain dear to me all my life, because on that chair and at that table he advanced from the playing with sand to a certificate of perfect maturity for the university.

Even into the common and neglected playing with sand we put much thought and reason. In educating a second child we would arrange many a thing to even better purpose. Yet I believe that a hint of what we did will do no harm. Mothers who will take the trouble, will be able to surpass us. So much the better!

Since occupations of this kind chiefly fall upon mothers, because pressing work keeps the father for hours at the desk, etc., I will let my wife tell what she did and how she proceeded in this matter.

The travel game, of which she will also report a specimen, will especially entertain and interest such children as have already traveled. And I wish with my whole soul that all children might do so, because nothing has such a deep and lasting influence as the frequent change of domicile and daily surroundings, especially if later one returns to the place where one abides. One then sees, hears, observes, thinks, judges, and concludes quite differently than before.

If such journeys are frequently and as objectively as possible brought back to memory by a playful imitation, so much the better. In this way the child remembers a hundred things and occurrences, which otherwise it would soon forget. It thus judges and compares them with greater acuteness.

Even very small journeys are strikingly useful, especially if they have been properly arranged and repeated. The rich in this respect are far better served than the poor. But let me now give his mother's account of some of her dealings with our child:

"Karl had a number of small kitchen-utensils for toys. As he was a great deal with me in the kitchen, and saw me prepare the dishes, I explaining everything to him, he was very much attracted by this occupation and began, at first in play, to imitate it. I soon helped him with it, guided him, and used the play, in order to give him better instruction in various things. Then we bought him larger and smaller vessels in which he, in the manner of our larder, kept his sand supplies. In one of the vessels he called the sand flour, in another rice, meal, salt, milk, etc.

"When the parts were distributed, he could choose whether he wanted to be mother or cook. If he represented the mother, he could order what he wanted to be cooked. I then asked a number of questions, and if he could not properly answer them, he lost his authority and became cook. Then I commanded, and I taught him what belonged to this dish or to that. For example, he had to bring soup-greens from the garden. If, as in the beginning was often the case, he brought the wrong greens, or could not remember a thing that he had been told several times, he was dismissed, after getting the reasons for such a dismissal.

"After that he could not so soon be cook again, but had to be satisfied to be a kitchen maid.

"We frequently played a kind of drama together, which gave him correct ideas about many circumstances of life.

"For example, he was mother and I the child. Then he gave his commands, which I at times carried out wrongly or not at all. If he missed noticing that, he lost his authority. But it was not often that he failed to see my pretended disobedience. On the contrary, he would make earnest and kind remonstrances. I promised I would improve, begged to be pardoned, but after a while started in again to do what I had been forbidden. If he noticed it, his droll earnestness caused me much pleasure. He threatened with severity, and occasionally would say, 'Yes, I see, you will not turn out well! I cannot love you any longer, poor mother that I am!'

"At times he was teacher and I the child. I purposely committed the same mistakes and transgressions of which he was guilty. He noticed them almost every time, and corrected and scolded me. In this way he felt most sensibly the disadvantages of his own mistakes, and learned how to avoid them. I could best cure him of his misdemeanors by committing them myself when he represented me.

"If he had been particularly good and bright, he was allowed to represent father. He then conversed with me, his wife, on all kinds of subjects, even of our son and his education, when he would make the most startling observations. Now and then I told him that I still noticed many faults in Karl, which I adduced one by one. He consoled me, and generally concluded with the words, 'Do not worry, my dear! Karl will turn out all right yet!'

"I frequently asked his advice about how I could cure the child of this or that, and he proposed all kinds of appropriate means. But when I replied to him, that I had already used them all, he answered emphatically, 'Well, if all that did not do any good, give him a spanking, so that he may think of it.'

"At other times we played the travel game. He had to tell me whither he was going to travel, what he wished to see on his journey, and whom he would visit. At the same time he mentioned by name the places through which he was traveling. These were indicated, in the winter in the room, in the summer in the garden, by some special object. Thus, for example, if he was traveling to Magdeburg, the chest of drawers represented Halle, the table—Kiennern, a chair—Bernburg, and the sofa—Magdeburg. I, not far away from it, seated on a chair, represented Pastor Glaubitz at Klein-Ottersleben, near Magdeburg.

"At first Karl made all the preparations for the journey, asking himself, for example, if he had taken all the necessary things with him, after which he departed from the stove, which stood for our home village of Lochau. Now he walked, now he rode on his hobby-horse, according to whether he, during his real journey, had found the road dry or muddy.

"If he fell in with several traveling companions, as had actually happened on the journey, he rode with them in his wagon.

"The time which he used for walking, riding, or driving, to the next station, was in every case proportioned to the distances of the places, the good or bad roads, the kinds of business or entertainments on the way, when I, naturally, would make remarks if he seemed to arrive too early or too late. He tried to correct me, and so forth.

"At Halle he visited Professor W., with whom he held a conversation. On the way to Koennern he stopped at an inn, ordered a sandwich and a glass of water, paid for it with slices of a turnip, then arrived at Koennern, where he visited the family H., to stay there over night.

"The next dinner he ate at Bernburg, where he called on several families. Then, an opportunity offering itself, he traveled to Magdeburg, and finally reached Klein-Ottersleben, where he told me, his friend Glaubitz, every noteworthy event of his journey. Such journeys were undertaken in every direction.

"If he had nothing worth while to tell, I would laughingly say:

'Send Peter through the world a-wandering—
What good it does? He can't recall a thing!'

"Then I was the traveler, when I told him a great many interesting things from the towns which we had both visited together. Thus we varied the game in every imaginable way.

"Now and then we both sat down at the table. I took the slate, and he was allowed to tell me what he wanted me to draw on it. 'A man!' would be the first thing he would call for. 'What next?' 'A house!' Then a cat, a tree, a dog, a child, and a table. When everything was put on the slate according to his wish, he wanted to know what the man's, child's, and dog's names were, and what they were doing there. I would then compose a story like this:

" 'The man's name, my child, is Peter Schultz, and he has just had this house built for himself. He used to be very poor, but he worked industriously and was saving. In this way he earned so much money that he was able to have the house built. Then he married a good, industrious girl, and after a while a child was born to his wife, and his name is August. His mother is just now in the kitchen, getting the dinner ready. Do you see the chimney smoking? Just a while ago she called her husband, asking him, since he was done with his work, to fetch August, who was playing under a tree, for dinner was ready. He might also bring in the dog and the cat, to get their dinner too. The good father did so, and as the weather was fine, he told mother, she might serve dinner in the garden, and so he brought the table out.' As a rule, he would repeat the story to his father at table, expressing, as he had already done to me, his misgivings about this or that, especially about the moral and spiritual conduct of the people of the tale, more particularly the children, we contradicting or agreeing with him."

It will be noticed that even poor people can use this method with all kinds of changes and improvements, in order to give their children a good time and instruct them.

One of the most profitable toys is a box of building blocks. Under intelligent guidance such blocks keep children busy and amuse them for many years, and they are able to learn a great deal by them. There are different kinds, some with which to imitate wooden buildings, others stone buildings. If those intended for wooden buildings, barns, stables, etc., were so arranged that they could be set up in many different ways, they would be very useful, especially in the country, where one sees almost exclusively wooden structures, for the child would be able more easily to imitate them. But, as a rule, only one single house can be constructed with them, and the parts have been too carefully indicated, so that a properly guided boy, who had been educated to think for himself, to seek and improve, soon gets tired of them. Still, they are useful in that they give the boy an objective idea of a wooden structure and its component parts.

If one is well-to-do enough to buy several of them, and, of course with the consent of the boy, rubs off the numbers indicating the corresponding parts, their usefulness is much increased thereby. One could also buy windmills and water-mills, as well as other imitations of important things which the child has seen, such as sluices, saltworks, steam-engines, etc.; but the main condition should be that they could all be taken to pieces and set up again. The directing numbers should also be removed at an early time.

If, in putting the parts wrongly together, something should get broken, father and child, and later on the child himself, should manage to fix it, and the child will thus invisibly be led to self-help and mechanical work.

Incomparably more important is a box of building-stones (made of wood). Those that I bought were an inch each way, some of them two, three, four, up to twelve inches long. Some of them were a quarter of an inch square, and six, eight, or twelve inches long, to be used in building the roof, as in ancient buildings.

We had, besides, keystones and obliquely cut stones, so that we could build a stone bridge with approaches. Nor was there any lack of stones for a breastwork.

With these Karl built everything, at first with my aid or the aid of his mother, then by himself: large and small houses, palaces (particularly such as he had seen), outhouses, barns, stables, bridges, churches, towers, fences, arbors, etc. Every building was provided with men, cattle, or utensils; the barns with corn or straw, the lofts with hay, the woodhouse with wood, the cellar and the larders with other things.

Hay and straw could be found in plenty; the garden furnished provisions, his mother gave them to him, or he himself took sand, earth, pebbles, and so forth. Men and animals were cut out of turnips, etc., and provided with wooden legs. The utensils were generally made of paper.

Karl was then master of the house. He had a wife, children, and servants; also horses, cows, sheep, pigs, chickens, geese, ducks, and so forth, which he attended to himself. He watched everything with great care. and kept in mind what was wanting.

One may easily understand what a wide, I may say what an immeasurable and yet highly fruitful, field is thus opened for parents and children. A properly brought-up child will pass hours each day building, for he will be thinking all the time, trying to discover something new, and instructing himself in a variety of ways.

Thus Karl once discovered the art of building with interstices, gaining thereby double and treble the use for his stones. His joy at this was very great, and his building operations increased immensely. Naturally we gave appropriate approval to his invention.

However few the toys were which Karl had, and however long the winter is in the country, Karl never became weary, nor was he ever tired of his toys. On the contrary, he was always merry and happy with them.

Most children get such a mass of toys to play with, that they all become a matter of indifference to them. Finally they do not pay the proper attention to anything, for they are satiated, keep demanding something new, something more expensive, only in order to have the things because they have seen other children with them. The proper use for these things, their helpfulness and the pleasure they should afford does not concern them.

They rather become indifferent toward what they have and greedy for what they do not own, and that is most injurious for their future lives. Their Christmas presents must end by becoming very expensive, and remain unused, whereas a few trifles, but such which could be put to various uses, gave Karl an incredible amount of pleasure.

As soon as the weather permitted, he lived in the open, under the circumstances described above. In the winter, especially during a clear frost, he played outside, walking, running, leaping, with all kinds of acrobatic variations, riding on a stick, pulling his cart or sleigh, as the case might be.

If the weather was more pleasant and the soil was no longer damp, the garden was his domicile. He passed hours in weeding, hunting for asparagus, comparing leaves and blossoms with one another; in finding out whether the plants and flowers were coming out and blossoming, in order to let us know about it; in observing the numberless insects, the creeping, running, hopping, flying ones, and to tell us about them later. He had no conception of fear of them. Even while he was an infant in our arms, we pointed them out to him as something attractive, told him about them, and got him used to them. We would say, "A boy must not be afraid!" and similar statements completed the instruction which we had started in the above-mentioned way.

If he found anything of the presence of which he thought we were ignorant, he brought it to us with a shout, asking insistently for instruction and eager to know what it was good for. He was particularly fond of birds. Their nests were almost as sacred to him as human habitations, and their young ones as children. He never got tired admiring the skilful and purposive structure of the nest; the faithful brooding of the bird; the care bestowed on the feeding of the young ones; their growth, change, fledging, flitting away, first accompanied by their parents, and then boldly and freely by themselves flying off into the world. All this gave him food for instruction.

How could we have been able to bring him up so Godfearing and pious without our yard, garden, meadow, and forest? The thought that God, not we, made everything grow and prosper, through sunshine, wind, rain, dew, mist, etc., was so strongly developed in him that he could not see a thing becoming green and blossoming without at the same time thinking of God the creator, father, preserver, and provider of all beings.

We, therefore, at times purposely varied the sentences, "It is growing, blossoming, bearing fruit," with the more correct ones, "God makes it grow, blossom, bear fruit." We particularly expressed ourselves thus in regard to the weather, whether it was good or bad for the crops.

If Karl was in the garden, or anywhere in the open, he felt himself to be in the earthly, visible kingdom of God, where the all-power, wisdom, and goodness of the Eternal One was ruling and daily working new miracles, most beneficent for man and beast. How could he have been able to think, speak or do anything wrong here, in the presence, under the eyes of his Heavenly Father!

"A child that has not yet been misguided," I maintain with full confidence, "will, under the above-mentioned circumstances always be and want to be Godfearing and Godloving, consequently obedient, respectful, and amiable, grateful, industrious, and so forth."

CHAPTER XIV

MUST CHILDREN PLAY MUCH WITH OTHER CHILDREN?

SINCE I was repeatedly informed that Karl should have a playmate, for otherwise he would not enjoy his childhood and would get tired, ill-humored, or even stubborn, I finally gave in and, with the aid of my wife, chose, one after the other, two somewhat grown girls who at that time were apparently the best-behaved children in the whole community. They sang, danced, and played with him, and he naturally was happy.

But the same child that heretofore had never been stubborn and had never told an untruth, now learned both. He also became accustomed to coarse expressions, and grew arbitrary and domineering, because these girls, who came to us on account of some small advantage to them, did not oppose him.

Our assurances that we should be happy if they did not give in to his will, but let us know of his arbitrariness, did no good. Their years, their social standing, their education, and the prejudices which are inseparable from it made them deaf against it, and we had to banish them.

It is indeed a foolish and highly injurious idea that children cannot be merry without other children.

It is only natural for them to wish to be with children, for with them they need not be so careful about their thoughts, inclinations, talks, and actions, and they are not guarded and supervised so constantly. But one need only be a child with them, need only take part in merry jests, let the children now and then get the upper hand and be more clever, by allowing them to occupy a place of greater dignity, and so forth, and they will feel just as happy playing with older persons, will learn to avoid naughty things, and will not so easily take any harm.

Worst of all it is to make playmates out of uneducated children, especially without any close observation. I have constantly found the troubles, which I mentioned in regard to Karl, repeated in other families as well, and even worse troubles. The virtues of the well-brought-up child pass over less readily to the ill-brought-up children than the faults of the latter infect the still unspoiled child, for virtues demand, at least in the beginning, effort and self-control, because they are contrary to our inclinations and passions. But faults are more easily adopted, because our sensuousness naturally leans that way, and the bad example of the little friend acts as an encouragement.

Most dangerous of all is the being together in an institution or public school. In regard to the latter it has been a settled principle for more than thirty years, observed by every sensible father, not to send his child, without the most urgent necessity, to the lower classes of the same, because there are more ill-brought-up children there than in the upper classes.

So long as our schools are not at the same time schools of moral training, so long as the pupils, from the first moment to the last (more especially in the recesses, as well as before and after school), are not constantly under the supervision of a teacher, the experienced father would gladly sacrifice all attendance at school, if the mass of information, which a large number of teachers can impart, did not make the instruction given by each of them in his specialty so desirable.

One ought to take but a very few children, say two or three, under one's charge, when the supervision could be made successful. If one, for financial reasons, wishes to take fifteen to twenty, one should keep enough teachers to have but two or three under the charge of one.

If none of these precautions have been taken, the faults which have been brought together from all the corners of the world must soon become the common possession, to outgrow and crush the few virtues which are present.

It is rank stupidity to imagine that children cannot be agreeable and sociable unless they all the time go around with other children. I have repeatedly found the very opposite to be the truth.

Karl and every child that was treated in the same way, were by that very treatment made more yielding, and it was, therefore, no hardship for them to have to yield. Other children tease what they want out of their playmates in various ways, and so become accustomed to self-assertion. From this there grow shrewdness, simulation, untruth, quarreling, stubbornness, hatred, envy, haughtiness, aspersion, fighting, calumniation, etc. A child remains quite free from all these, so long as he plays only with his parents or with other sensible persons.

Naturally the opportunity for coming together with children is not excluded, but their commingling should occur only now and then, and under supervision. Such an occasional meeting, when all the reserve has not been thrown off, can do no harm. Karl has had many a chance for meeting children under such circumstances during his longer or shorter journeys.

He got along so well with them that they invariably became very fond of him and nearly always parted from him with tears in their eyes. Having become accustomed to calm, merriment, order, and sensible reasoning, even in his games, he observed these virtues also when with other children. There was for him no ready cause for quarreling. On the contrary, he frequently avoided it by clearing away misunderstandings, or put an end to it by prayers, sensible arguments, and so forth.

Since he never quarreled at home with any

one, such action appeared to him repulsive and unseemly. He felt that quarreling put an end to playing, nor was his blood roused by daily recurring quarrels. He consequently did not so easily become excited, nor did his blood boil as easily as that of children constantly quarreling and fighting with one another. He knew nothing of that anger which so frequently puts an end to children's playing. He remained calm, while others grew excited. Not even the naughtiest of boys could ever have brought him so far as to make him swear or fight.

Nearly all the children, boys and girls, who knew him more intimately became fond of him. There was but one opinion about him, that he was very amiable and could get along well with others. I do not know a single case, not even in his maturer years, of his having quarreled with one of his many youthful friends, or of having fallen out with them, although many an occasion offered itself for it during his investigation, and even lively discussion, of learned subjects. I may say there should have been such occasions, because his opponents were usually considerably older than he.

He generally sided with his betters, and these betters knew him well, hence that intimate respect and love which they still have for him. Their mutual relations have frequently moved me to tears.

My thanks are due to these worthy young men for having so tenderly and lastingly clung to him. They are sure of my respect and of his.

People would, therefore, do well to drop that harmful prejudice that children can be made happy and merry only by playing with other children. With the same right one may say that they should be left much in the company of the servants, for they like to be in their company for similar reasons, whereas, who would be so rash as to abandon them to servants, except in a case of dire necessity?

CHAPTER XV

KARL'S DIET

MY wife scarcely changed her usual manner of life during her pregnancy. She at best avoided the heavy vegetables, or ate a little less of them than usual. She proceeded in the same manner all the time she nursed Karl.

People knew that we would take no wet nurse and that Karl was going to have no other food than his mother's milk, if she should have enough nourishment for him. So they expressed their anxiety for us and for Karl. For, they said, the mother is not big and strong; how, then, can she give sufficient to the child?

Then there began to pour in advice which, if I had been unreasonable or weak enough to follow it, would have made my wife ill and would have killed my son, or would have made a weakling of him.

Imagine a person who, as all the advisers well knew, had never eaten anything but the ordinary articles of food used in our station of life; who never drank anything but pure water, although she frequently could have had all costly beverages for nothing; whose breakfast consisted of bread and butter and a glass of water, while walking with me through the garden; who never drank tea or coffee in the afternoon, and in the evening ate something very simple, and—mind you—had been brought up in this manner of life, felt particularly well and happy with it; imagine a person like this all of a sudden exhorted "in the morning to take in bed two cups of very strong coffee with excellent cream, and to eat a pretzel or something like it; at ten o'clock to drink one large cup or two small cups of strong chocolate and eat with it a roll toasted in butter."

If she had any appetite before dinner, or if it was still long to dinner, she was "to have a cup or two of good meat broth." At dinner "she should have nothing but strengthening meat soup, fine vegetables, roast of chicken, duck, or venison, with something nourishing or refreshing, a few glasses of old French wine or very good red wine, whose quality should be carefully tested," while during the whole day she should have "very strong beer, best of all Morseburg beer with sugar." After dinner again "a few cups of particularly good coffee with cream; between five and six o'clock a few cups of tea with pretzels, or good meat broth; and in the evening meat-soup with some roast." With this a glass of wine, and after it the beer, as described. She must "abstain from all housework, must not run around so much, but may walk about the garden now and then."

If my wife had, by some kind of a miracle, survived such a manner of life and remained in good health, Karl would have become a roly-poly, keeping his mother awake at nights with his restlessness, suffering from teething, and going through all kinds of children's diseases with their frequently injurious consequences. But, with God's aid, nothing of the kind was to happen, if my attending of medical lectures and later careful observation and experience were to count for anything.

However much my inexperienced wife may have felt inclined to follow the manner of life which had been recommended to her, I must do her the justice of stating that, relying upon me, she rejected it in the whole and in its parts, and continued her usual way of living, paying, as before, attention to her household duties, and doing plenty of running about. It does her double honor, because she might have embarrassed me with the common saw, "Everybody says so; do you pretend to know better than everybody?" It did not escape my notice that, as a human creature, she occasionally thought that way. But she very rarely gave utterance to it, for an experience of nearly four years had shown her that there was reason in my simple treatment of the human body.

The only change she made in her manner of living was that in the morning and evening she ate some thin oatmeal gruel and at dinner took a little more soup than usual. Consequently the milk came in without the least disturbance, and she knew of milk fever and such like only from hearsay. Besides, she always had enough nourishment for Karl, so that he did not need any other food, yet was well fed. So much a pure, unspoilt human organism may perform, and so little does it need! Of puerperal fever, etc., there was not even a thought.

But how easily my wife might have gotten

it, and how surely our child would have been sacrificed, if we had paid attention to the advice urged on us, is proved by the following:

At a christening at K., where my wife was as happy as usual and had a good appetite, she found a meat dish which she liked in particular and so ate in the evening of it more than was good for her. She was perfectly well the next day, but her milk did not preserve the customary mildness to which Karl had become accustomed. So he got a little heat and a slight fever. Instead of any medicine for him, his mother partook that day of considerably less meat, ate light food, and took a longer walk under God's free heaven. This cured Karl, and the next day he was as well as a fish in the water.

Had we not observed his illness and correctly judged its cause, and had we, in consequence, tried to cure it by means of medicine, that is, by some kind of poison, while my wife continued to feed on heavy meats, what then?

But our advisers did not consider such things, or, rather, did not want to consider them, but were sure, as so many men are, that their advice was unfailing, and that we should have to follow it, if we had any respect for them. In their shortsightedness these people confused the concepts "advice" and "command" with one another. I have often observed and painfully felt such confusion in professional scholars.

I have never understood the art of saying "Yes!" and doing "No!" So I tried at first to persuade my advisers that it would be better to follow a different course from that which they advocated. But I failed completely in convincing them. Immediately, as usual, calumnies began to scatter from Dieskau, over Halle, in all directions where I was known, accusing me of being quarrelsome, haughty, vain, stingy, mean to my wife, and asserting that I pretended to know everything better than anybody else. Openly, indeed, my detractors voiced their belief that my wife would grow weak and that my son would thus die. But when neither happened, when all secret and public inquiries proved to my antagonists, to their regret, that I was right, they became even more provoked against me, and now condemned me in general, where before they had condemned me in relation to particular things.

From that time dates the statement, which for many years has been made in regard to me at Halle, that I was a favorite of Fate, for the critics would not admit that the success of this or that plan was the result of ripe experience, much thought, and iron persistency.

Karl was nursed for nine months, getting no other food during that time. Only once did I from human weakness submit to the general assurance that the mother would be too much affected by it. We tried carefully to feed Karl additionally, but mother and child at once began to suffer from it, and we returned to our better ways.

When he was to be weaned, we gave him now and then a little soup of powdered toast with water and a little butter. By degrees we repeated the experiment more frequently, while my wife kept more and more away from the child. After a few days he forgot about the nursing, and his mother lost the milk, without knowing how.

Now the above-mentioned soup began more frequently to alternate with oatmeal gruel, and occasionally my wife boiled the oatmeal with fresh milk. A little later he now and then got a little meat soup, which we thinned with water, if it appeared to us to be too strong. By degrees he was accustomed to light vegetables, finally to everything which we ourselves ate, excepting that we gave him comparatively little meat. In consequence of this natural procedure he got one tooth after the other, without any pain and without our knowing it.

The loss of the milk in my wife was prepared in the following manner: From the time that Karl was to be weaned she ate considerably less, least of all meat and nourishing dishes, so that at times she was really hungry, and she drank much water. In this way the milk became visibly thinner, ran out, when Karl did not drink it, and completely stopped in a few days, without the slightest pain.

In the first two years the boy received in the morning some soup, later on the same food as we took, bread and butter and fresh water. Up to his fourth year or so we gave him a second piece of bread and butter between ten and eleven o'clock.

In spite of our strict attention, the child occasionally received something in secret, especially from the peasant women, because these know of no other way of expressing their love. Once he might have been greatly harmed in this way, for Mrs. P. G. at R. had fed him with blood sausage, while he was still being nursed. We found that out next day from the servant who had taken him there, when Karl had become ill.

Beginning with his third year his food was precisely the same as ours. After his simple breakfast and constant motion in the open, he generally had an excellent appetite for his dinner. He was taught to eat everything. We here united love with earnestness and reason, as in his whole educational scheme. Our dishes were cooked fresh every day, and they were well prepared. If there was one which he did not particularly like, we made this concession that we did not force him to eat much of it. At the same time we directed his attention, by representations or a story invented for the occasion, to the fact that by his dislike he deprived himself of a great enjoyment, since the particular food was very much liked by us and by all other men. "We rejoice every time it comes," we would say, "and you feel grieved! Get used to eating it, and you will not be grieved, but will rejoice with us!" Since we, his parents, ate anything, we could so much the more easily get him to do likewise, by directing his attention to our example. In fact, in a very short time he ate everything.

At four o'clock he got his bread and butter, and drank a small pot of water. Frequently he would do without the butter, because our stories had taught him the usefulness of reducing one's wants. In the evening he received his soup, as a rule before our supper, so that he could go to bed in good season.

We cannot recall a case when he had an attack of indigestion while living at home. Even when away from home, that happened but rarely and was not of much importance. His hosts would stuff him, from so-called love. But as soon as he had come to his senses, he refused to accept such manifestations of love, and, even when the most attractive dainties were offered him, would say, to their astonishment and even anger, "I thank you, I have had enough!"

I aver most solemnly that the silly love for Karl went so far that people of that type bore me a real grudge, because they could not see, and therefore could not admit, that Karl's refusals came from his soul.

"It is against nature," they would say, "for a child not to like dainties. You must have forbidden him with great severity to eat them, or you must have signaled to him and the poor boy obeys you implicitly!"

Such, forsooth, were the words that were uttered in my presence and that of Karl. It was a settled thing with them that I was a barbarian.

The dear people naturally spoke of nature as viewed from their standpoint, and did not even suspect that it is the business of the educator to ennoble the lower, sensuous nature, that it is his duty to elicit what is highest in man by means of reason and habit, to strengthen it, and to make it occupy a commanding position. Still less did they know that it was an easy matter to accomplish, and that in a child properly brought up from the start the result came of its own accord.

Having been in a hundred different ways instructed in the matter, Karl considered health and good spirits to be two invaluable possessions. We seldom or never allowed an opportunity to pass without lauding them and regretting their absence. "He who eats too much," we would often say, "later loses his good spirits and grows indisposed and even sick." If he had been overfed at some place, we pitied him, because he had to suffer, could not be as happy as usual; in a lively manner, yet truthfully, we brought before his eyes the many inconveniences which he now had to suffer; directed his attention to the possible, even worse consequences; reminded him, especially in good weather, of his loss at not being able to play outside, or study, or help us; made him observe that we, too, on his account, could not be outside, that we missed some things and were worried.

How could a child whose mind and heart had been properly trained help hearing all that with sorrow? If I know anything about the human mind, he could not help regretting his imprudence and make up his mind to be more cautious in the future. Excuses such as, "They pushed it upon me," were not accepted, and so they were never given by Karl.

"You know, dear child, that it is injurious to eat more than is absolutely necessary. Why did you give in? Will they now be suffering for you? Go and ask them to! But you cannot do that, and they cannot and will not take over your pain. So be more careful in the future, and on such occasions think of our injunction! Or do you believe that they know better than we? Do you imagine they love you more than we do? Dear boy, how could that be possible? We, your parents, who give you every day so many proofs of our love and care! No, my child, you cannot imagine that! The food which you ate elsewhere does not cost us anything,—then why do we so earnestly wish you had not eaten it? Because it hurts you!"

Deeply touched, he would embrace us and give the most solemn promise that he would in the future watch himself more closely.

As a rule we told him afterward a story or two invented for the occasion, and these never failed in their purpose. We also drew examples from life, for which, alas, only too many cases offered themselves. Among the peasant children overeating is unfortunately a common occurrence, for these people cling to sensuality, because the higher enjoyments are unknown and unattainable by them. We preferably drew his attention to similar incidents in more cultured families, especially if they referred to some young friend or acquaintance.

The son of a pastor not far away was named F. The child was one year old when I entered the house of his parents for the first time. He was such a pretty boy that on my way home to Lochau I said to my wife, "That child could be trained very highly!"

But the boy was soon named "gold son," "father's treasure," "mother's treasure," and so forth (he, certainly, was the last two, but not the first), and before long I came to the conviction that the child could not be trained so highly after all. The child was so stuffed that he became big and fat. His mother frequently showed him to us with a certain pride, because he was such a butterball. I felt really anxious about him, and so I could not keep from explaining to her the dangers which awaited such a well-fed baby.

But she smiled with a knowing mien, and the father with self-satisfaction pointed to his remaining nine children, who, it is true, had "grown." As I could not discuss this particular point, I kept silent.

What I feared actually happened. The child suffered from time to time from his excessive feeding, grew daily more homely, suffered excruciating toothaches, got all kinds of children's diseases, and was often near death. But as his parents were very healthy, he, too, had much vitality; so he went on suffering, and survived.

When the boy was eight or nine years old, I could never look at him without sorrow,—he was small, bloated, repellent in shape, with an uncommonly large head, the face pitted from smallpox, his features irregular, his eyes dimmed, his expression dull.

It is to be lamented that men so frequently tread humanity under foot. The little creature had no time for reasoning,—he was all the time busy with his digestion. His mentality was therefore in a most pitiable condition. But he did not know it. In the village school, which he attended off and on, he was far behind the peasant children, but these respected him as the pastor's child, and so he felt his distance from them in an inverse sense.

I was so fully convinced that he gorged himself at every holiday, that once, soon after Christmas, I asked his elder brother, whom we met on a walk:

"How is everybody at home? All are well?"

"Thank you, yes!"

"But F. is sick, is he not?"

"Yes, he is. But how do you know it already?"

"O well! Is it not just after Christmas?"

The humanely inclined person will comprehend with what bitter feeling I voluntarily uttered those words. But I risked very little, for this elder son had also eaten a great deal during his childhood.

I went at once with Karl to see F. He had violent abdominal pain and a very violent headache, and was delirious.

I led the whole conversation, in Karl's presence, by means of questions and answers, in such a way that everything was discussed as I wanted, and that Karl carried away more than enough for himself. Then I pitied the victim of imprudence from the fullness of my heart, wished him a speedy recovery, and returned home.

No sooner were we in the open than Karl went over everything he had heard and seen with me, accompanying everything with appropriate remarks. He earnestly begged me to keep him in the future from overeating, and on his part promised absolute obedience.

In this way we soon needed only to give

him a little warning, whenever we went out calling, and even this could after a while be dispensed with.

What could I have done with him, if he had not been brought up in that manner? Even in his fourth, fifth, and sixth year he used to sit in Magdeburg, Leipsic, Dresden, Berlin, and Rostock, but especially in small cities and villages, at well-filled tables, and frequently a great distance away from me, some person or other having asked for his company at table. When, in his seventh, eighth, and ninth year, he became well known, he would have perished, for we were then invited to the tables of the rich. On such occasions Karl was separated far from me, in order to be under observation, and they confessed to me more than once that they had in vain tried to tempt him.

At first this caused me anxiety, but later on I only smiled and remained calm, because from his fifth year he had been eating at home without restraint, according to his inclination, and yet had never overeaten.

In regard to sugar and all sweetmeats, we had taught him from the start to eat but little or nothing at all of them. Sugar and sweetmeats give the children a sweet tooth, and then they become indifferent toward simple dishes. This is bad enough, but they soon hanker for the sugared dainties, which they buy for themselves. That is worse. If they cannot buy any more, they become dissatisfied with their parents and their circumstances, and perhaps steal the sweetmeats or the money for them. Which decidedly is worst of all.

Besides, I believe that the frequent use of sweetmeats coats the stomach and, since the sweetmeats are generally also rich, ruins it. This creates or, rather, breeds worms, producing untold annoyance, even horrible cramps. Nor can the sugar taken in great quantity and bitten into, as children always do, help being injurious to the young teeth, since it contains a strong salt, which directly injures the enamel and the tooth itself, with its nerves. Even if this were not the case, the exhalations of the stomach, coated and ruined by the sweetmeats, are enough to spoil the child's teeth. I have always found it so, and I have observed the beneficial consequences of a contrary treatment.

I will also mention that sweetmeats are generally given to children when their hunger has already been satisfied, and that consequently this alone must be injurious, causing a spoiled stomach, because sweetmeats stimulate one to eat more than one otherwise would.

In any case I have found the popular prejudice justified. "Sweetmeats give the children black teeth," and "Sugar makes the teeth fall out."

So Karl was never allowed to fall into the habit of eating either much sugar or many sweetmeats. Others pressed them on him, but in vain.

In a Halle family it was the custom to give the children off and on a cone of candy. I begged them not to give one to Karl, but it did no good. I elaborated my reasons, but they were laughed away. I was thinking of ceasing to visit this house or, at least, letting Karl appear there less frequently, but this proved unnecessary. Karl understood us so well that he divided the cone among us and other persons present, and with the sugar, of which they also gave him large pieces, he fed a dog, who was very fond of it. The surprising thing was that he never gave the sugar to a human being, as though he considered it unworthy of a man to eat sugar.

I suffered many an annoyance from that family, who otherwise were kindly inclined toward me. Every time Karl divided up his candy or fed the dog, he was scolded for it, and I was even asked to order him to keep what he was given. I would nct have done so for anything in the world. At first that considerably disturbed the social merriment, but by degrees our hosts became accustomed to it. When Karl was in his third year and persisted in his determination not to eat the candy, they completely stopped urging him or me.

It has been mentioned that Karl ate comparatively little meat. This practice was long continued, but his rations were increased from year to year, especially when we noticed that he was growing more than usual, or when we had some other reason for assuming that more nourishing food would be good for him.

For this purpose we noted every day, often more than once a dav, Karl's complexion, appetite, activity, and spirits,—and also, later, the ease with which his mind worked, but more especially his growth. His height was marked on a door-post. He was measured the first of each month, and as a rule the increase in height was noticeable every time. If it was greater than usual, we gave him a little more meat.

It needs no proof that much meat is injurious to the stomach and the intestines of children. It putrefies with the least disorder to which they are subjected, and ruins the purity of the juices, from which various troubles naturally result.

Even if the children digest it all and develop no visible bodily ailment, it still injures them, for they become violent, arbitrary, stubborn, cruel, and so forth.

This lies in the nature of things, and is shown by the wildness of the purely meat-eating animals and the greater mildness of the purely plant-eating animals. I have found the same to be the case with men as well, and all the information we have of distant peoples agrees with my personal observation. We had a convincing example, in the case of Karl, that an entirely vegetable diet made a child almost too meek and yielding. I consider it my duty to report the case, especially as the contrary deduction in the opposite case may thus be safely made.

By means of careful treatment and diet

Karl, in his third year, as ever afterward, was neither too violent, nor too meek. At that time I decided, for sufficient reasons, to make a visit to Hamburg with my wife. Our great question was not what would in the meanwhile become of our property, but what we should do with Karl.

Many persons expressed the wish to take Karl to their house while we were away. But we were afraid, here of the sugar, there of the meat, or of too great indulgence, and so wavered for a long time. At last we decided to intrust him to our now deceased friend and relative, Merchant J. H. Heintz in Leipsic. He had proved that he knew how to bring up children, for his three sons and two daughters, all grown, did him the greatest honor. Besides, he was the one person who most closely agreed with my method of education. In his house, where we visited frequently, Karl was never tempted to any of the above-mentioned indulgences.

Heintz was perfectly willing to take Karl into his house, but demanded detailed written instructions as to how he and his family should treat the child. I gave them to him, but, perhaps, dwelt too much on the point that Karl should get but little meat, or else he and his family, from noble conscientiousness, took me too closely at my word. Anyway, Karl in those eight weeks that he was with them, out of amiable precaution did not get enough meat. When we called for him, we were moved almost to tears by his excessive meekness. The formerly lively, kindly yet droll, roguish, nay, at times even wanton boy had completely disappeared. Before us stood a soft, yielding, gently smiling being, who at first did not recognize us, and then doubtfully and weakly responded to our ardent embraces with a tear in his eye.

That very day, while still in Leipsic, I gave him a little more meat than customary, and we went back to Lochau. In two weeks he was tumbling about merrily in the house, in the yard, and in the garden; was as much of a rogue as before; and again knew how, in jest, to tease.

CHAPTER XVI

WHAT WE DID FOR KARL'S MORAL EDUCATION

THE fundamental rules which we followed for Karl's moral development, and tried to execute with the greatest conscientiousness, were these: Always to be just and reasonable, stern but amiable toward him. If one of us had overlooked something in him or had too easily forgiven him, the other considered that to be as great a fault as to have been too stern or too vehement, for, at bottom, both are equally bad.

Karl was allowed to ask for anything that was natural, that was not unjust, that was good. It was generally granted to him, even if we had to add the remark that, for this reason or that, it was no longer proper for him. If he asked for anything else, he was flatly refused it, without giving him any further reasons, if he could know them himself; with sound and comprehensible reasons, if they were still unknown to him. If he seemed to have forgotten those which he knew, we quizzed him, to bring them back to his memory.

Even in his first year we used to say, loudly, clearly, and earnestly, "No!" Then, perhaps, would rattle with two keys, or show him something new, saying, with emphasis, "Look, Karl!" He generally looked at what we held before him, listened to our words, and thus forgot what he wanted.

It is self-understood that such a helpless creature could not be allowed to suffer any want in food and drink, in cleanliness and order, for otherwise he would not have been satisfied with the rattling of the keys, for the bodily want would have returned the moment the curiosity was satisfied. But I dare say that our child never suffered in that direction.

After a short time we hardly needed to do anything more than turn his attention to some other thing, for he soon noticed that "Yes!" with us meant "Yes!" and "No" meant "No!" whether he afterward cried or laughed. Thus he imperceptibly became accustomed to obey implicitly, and I can aver that we had nothing to desire in this respect, until we took some boys to our house to educate.

Implicit obedience is infinitely more important than one would usually think, for a child is again and again on the point of doing something by which he may hurt himself. To the obedient child you need only call out, "Do not do that, my child!" or simply call him by name, and he will stop at once, will stand still, will pay attention, and so forth. Then you can impart to him the reasons for the prohibition, in order to safeguard the child in a future similar situation. You may call to a disobedient child as loudly as you wish. Not being in the habit of obeying, he will go on doing what he wanted, and then it is too late, for the damage has been done.

One incident will serve as an example and proof of the freedom of action which Karl enjoyed and in which he was protected against everybody. In the nature of things his mother was in the first two or three years of his lifé dearer to him than I. I was much in my study, out on business, or away from the house. When I was in his presence, I earnestly, nay, severely, insisted upon order, cleanliness, obedience, etc., and thus obtained things which his mother, as a feminine being, either was not able to obtain or, from motherly love or even carelessness, had overlooked.

The little fellow could not grasp my attitude yet, nor recognize the justice and paternal amiability in it all. Hence he loved his mother more than me. I had long noticed it, but I was satisfied, for it seemed natural to me. Once we were sitting all three on a sofa, and Karl was playing most tenderly with my wife. But she, in the goodness of her heart, kept pointing to my side, and the child turned to fondle me also, but immediately went back to his mother. She shoved him once more over to my side, whispering to him to be more tender toward me. I immediately addressed her with much earnestness:

"For the Lord's sake, let him fondle whomsoever he wishes, for it is right so! He now loves you more than me, and he must, if I am not to reprove him. He cannot help manifesting it unless he is a hypocrite. But the time will come, when I will do more for him than you. Then he will certainly honor me, if not love me, more."

My wife understood me. She gave him his will, and that time has actually come.

So far as it was in any way possible, I tried to keep his judgments pure and free. The thousands of prejudices pro and con, which are inculcated in the ordinary education, cling to people to their graves, and immeasurably interfere with their clear perception in the affairs and incidents of life.

I know full well that one must not speak at all with children about certain things, while other things should be mentioned only with great caution and reserve, and other things again should not be broached until they have formed and expressed their own opinion about them. But then their opinion should not be lied away, in so far as it is right. I will only grant this much, that it may be somewhat softened, with the use of the greatest caution, so that its rough edges shall be polished off.

If Karl, as a child, passed in society a correct but too abrupt or harsh a judgment, I let it stand, but said to the persons present, in half jest, "You see, he is a village boy! You must not take it ill of him!"

Karl soon came to understand that he had in such cases uttered a correct but improper statement, and he was sure, when we were alone, to ask me the "Why?" of it. Then I had a good opportunity to show him the pros and cons of the case, and to get him used to better manners, without narrowing his intellect or doing his heart any injury. Above all I tried, whenever possible, to refer it to a higher morality and to true piety. In such a case I would calmly say:

"Your judgment was strictly correct, but though I must acknowledge this, it was not good or kind of you to utter it. You should hardly have spoken it in the presence of your parents, and never in the presence of others. Did you observe how embarrassed Mr. N. was? He could not, or would not, contradict, perhaps from love and respect for us, but he was much hurt to have a child tell him something unpleasant. If he is out of sorts to-day or others make fun of him, you are to be blamed for it!"

Karl was certainly moved by this deeply, and was truly sorry for having pained him. But let us suppose Karl did not see his mistake and, instead, answered, "But he was friendly with me all the time," I should then have replied:

"Perhaps from pity for you, because my

words, 'He is a village boy,' showed him the real state of affairs. You have certainly not gained respect, love, and gratitude for yourself by your embarrassing judgment. You do not seem to have noticed that the persons present anxiously watched, now you, now me, now him, and the conversation would have halted, if I had not turned it to something else that attracted them vividly."

I again assume the truly unthinkable case that Karl was still not ashamed, but would have answered, "But it was true!" I would have corrected him more earnestly:

"Are you sure about that? It may very well be that you are mistaken. How if he had answered, 'A reason with which you are not acquainted compelled me to act that way.' How then? Or if he had said to you, 'Are you my judge? You, a little, unreasoning child?' Even if it was true, unconditionally true, his statement being wrong,—which I, however, still doubt,—ought you not have kept silence from consideration for him? Did you not observe that we were all silent? Or are you so simple as to believe that you alone noticed the mistake in his actions?

"Tell me, my child, how would you like

it, if he, and a hundred others, should take you up for your oversights, weaknesses, carelessness, blunders, and so forth, and should even lay them before the eyes of strangers? And that would be a mere trifle, for it would be a grown man who would reprove a child, which would be perfectly proper and unquestionably right. The child would not be harmed by such a reproof, for from an unreasoning being like you people expect a lot of things which are not just right, and they pass over them lightly, or pardon them altogether.

"Or do you imagine that other people do not observe your mistakes? You are wrong there! Out of kindness toward you, or, perhaps, toward others as well, they pass over them in silence and do not embarrass you by mentioning them to you. But several of my friends, who love you sincerely, have often told me or your mother of incidents which do you no honor. They did not tell about them to any one else, and they told them to us only because they wished to improve and ennoble you.

"This noble kindness pleases you, does it not? Very well, then you must act in the same manner. 'What you wish that people should do to you, you must do first to them!'

"To tell the truth, to tell it in a harsh and provoking manner, to be severely just and painfully search out the faults of your fellow-man, or even reprove him for them, without any particular reason for it, in the presence of others, is far removed from being good, yet being good is something unspeakably beautiful, for we call for this very reason the sum of all perfection 'God,' that is, 'Good.' You, too, my child, wish to become like God. If you do, you must perfect yourself as much as possible. Above all, do not forget to be good."

I am sure that by that time Karl would have promised, with tears of contrition, never again to pain a person in that manner, and I am convinced that only human, more particularly childish, weakness could ever have led him to do so.

But for my purpose I will assume that, none the less, he will retort, "Shall I tell an untruth?" Assuming this, I would have replied:

"Not in the least! For then you would be lying or be a hypocrite. But there is no need of all that. All you have to do is to keep quiet. It would, indeed, be a sad life for you, for me, and for all men, if everybody were to search out the faults or foibles of his acquaintances, and ruthlessly tell of them before others. That would be an eternal war of all against all, for no man is without faults. No one would be at rest. Everybody would have to be constantly on the watch, in order to strike or to protect himself. Would that be living with each other as men, as Christians, as children of one father, as representatives of the highest Good?"

But I do the poor boy an injustice. It may be that I have told him all that, but, I am sure, never at one time, for so much was not necessary to cause him to perceive, regret, and mend faults against morality or piety. I have, however, forgotten to mention that I would also have told him some appropriate story, which indeed the reader will surmise, from previous hints.

CHAPTER XVII

How Karl Learned to Read and Write

One of Karl's favorite amusements was to look at pictures. We naturally explained to him everything worth knowing in a picture, and afterward we had him describe it to us, now as his teachers, now as his pupils. So long as he could not read, we used to say regretfully:

"Oh, if you only knew how to read! It is a most interesting story, but I have no time to tell it to you."

If we then went away, he looked at the story in the picture-book as at a talisman whose secret powers were useless to him, because he lacked the magic word with which to unlock it. At times he would create for himself another story from the picture, which he related to us in order that we might give him the real story.[1] Thus we roused in him by degrees the desire for reading.

[1] The telling of stories was indeed an essential part of Karl's early education, and I cannot sufficiently recommend

Meanwhile I bought Basedow's elementary work, with the explanatory text, then a number of other appropriate readers with etchings. I must remark here that many of these unfortunately were borrowed from Basedow, and often were inferior to those in his book. However, since I myself had a fairly large collection of etchings, from which I from time to time selected what was appropriate for Karl's observation, he generally had a sufficient supply of pictures during the rough season. In good weather, Nature, or what we saw on our journeys, and in the evening the starred heavens, were his picture-book. This turning from one to another, from books to life, was of incalculable value to the child.

When we got so far as to have Karl express a desire to learn reading—he was then

it to other parents—particularly the invention and telling of stories to inculcate specially needed lessons Such stories, properly told, are not readily forgotten by a child. At times, if Karl acted like some bad boy of whom he had heard a story, we only needed briefly and emphatically to say, "Martin," or "Peter," and he understood perfectly. I would also recommend the learning by heart of short poems, which, however, should be readily comprehensible One may begin with, "Children, how great all the Pleasures will be," or with "When I am good," and by gradually giving more difficult poems one may in a short time reach Schiller The child will understand everything, and his mind, morality, piety, taste, conduct, and memory will thus be trained between three and four years old—I bought in Leipsic ten sets of the German printed letters, large and small, similarly ten sets of the Latin alphabet, of the diacritical and other marks, and of the numbers from 0 to 9. Every letter was three inches high and pasted on a piece of wood. I threw the whole into a box, and showed it to him as a new game, the letter game.

Then all three of us sat down on the carpet, fished out the German small letters, mixed them all up, and blindly picked up one of them. The letter so taken up was carefully and solemnly surveyed and loudly and distinctly named. It went from hand to hand, and everybody did the same. At first we so arranged it that only the vowels, a, e, or i, etc., would reappear frequently. We then held each before Karl, before naming it ourselves, and if he recognized it, we fondled him. If he did not recognize it, we would laughingly say, "Oh, you silly child, it is an a or e," etc.

I assure you, it took but a few days, and only a few quarters of an hour each day, for Karl to know all the letters.

The German capital letters were introduced now and then, as if by accident. Now my wife asked me, now I my wife, now Karl one of us, to look carefully at the capital and tell how it differed from the corresponding small letter. This may be varied at will.

When he had mastered both kinds of letters, I secretly threw in a few of the Latin small letters. If one of them made its appearance, it was admired and ridiculed in common for having lost its way among the German letters. Karl had to look for the corresponding German letter and to compare the two. In this way he very soon learned the Latin small letters, after which the next step, to the Latin capitals, was very easy, especially as he began to play with the letters by himself.

As soon as he had learned the letters, we began to put together syllables and words. We naturally chose as funny ones as we could, or let him choose them. At other times, some friend of ours would ask Karl to teach him the letter game, pretending that he did not know it, or, as a reward for some good action of the child, he offered to play the game with him. Thus we rearranged the instruction in many ways, and in a short and easy manner attained what we wished, without really teaching him reading.

He knew all the letters perfectly; he formed syllables and words from them quite correctly and without any labor; he even composed sentences. He had also learned the marks and the numbers, and knew how to use them. That was all I wanted for the time being, as I was afraid of precocity. Now, when Karl was four years old, I visited, with my friends Glaubitz and Tillich, the Pestalozzi Institute and traveled at the same time through Switzerland and Upper Italy. My wife, who was always afraid that Karl, on account of his mediocre ability, would not learn much, and who saw with anxiety how little I, apparently, was doing for him, used my long absence to teach him to read, as she wished to surprise me with his accomplishment.

What I had feared actually happened. The child, who heretofore had learned everything from Nature, from his surroundings, and from illustrations, using the little objects, such as building-blocks and letters only as a game, became considerably embarrassed and discouraged when he had to busy himself with mere printed words, of which four, six, or even eight in a row made no sense at all or no attractive sense whatsoever.

The letters from which Karl had been in the habit of forming his own words, or those funny ones which we made for him to pronounce, had been three inches in height, while those which were not at all entertaining were only a line in size. All that displeased him, and made his mother's instruction very hard. Thank Heaven that it did not entirely discourage Karl.

When I returned, Louise had by dint of hard work gotten him to read laboriously. I acknowledged her good-will gratefully, but in reality put little value upon what she had accomplished, because Karl was not to have such instruction as yet, partly because I had not yet noticed in him any lively desire to read in books. I was afraid that general instruction would annoy him, when I heard him refuse to read a short story, even though we assured him that it was funny and would amuse him. "I thank you," he said, "I do not want to read it, I know it already."

I would easily have been persuaded into allowing him to forget the whole laboriously acquired art of reading, but that would have pained my wife. At that very time I was writing about the Pestalozzi Institute and thinking a great deal about the teaching and learning of reading. I was thus induced to search for all kinds of means for making reading agreeable to Karl, so that he would be able quickly and with pleasure to enjoy the fruits of his endeavor; and I was uncommonly happy when I found a few very short, and yet droll stories, which he liked to read and which he of his own accord frequently read to us, with a merry laugh. "Do you see," I said, "what a pleasure it is to be able to read? See what pleasure you will have from it soon, in the winter, when you cannot play in the open!" Our friends, too, asked him to amuse them by reading to them, and thus I attained what I wanted. He became fonder and fonder of it, and it was not long before I could purchase appropriate books for him. He read them eagerly, some of them two and three times.

I have already spoken of his correct intonation. His reading facility he owed to himself, for it was a rule with me (1) to instill him with love for his study, (2) to teach him the most necessary thing, (3) to make the instruction as comprehensible and easy as possible. After all that had been obtained, we, his parents, with the occasional help of our friends, merely encouraged, furnished the opportunity, praised, and rewarded him. He did the rest himself.

I should have, indeed, had too much to do, if, with my official duties, with the many things which I then had to prepare for the printer, and with the frequent journeys devolving on me, I had tried to carry to completion the child's education. That would have by far surpassed my time, strength, and desire, and, besides, would have been entirely against my plan.

For the same reason I did not formally teach Karl writing. We frequently spoke to one another, to him, and to others, in his presence, of the great usefulness of writing, and we frequently gave him inducements for the desire to write. But we did not help him out, at least not for any length of time, and only after his repeated requests. At first he drew the printed letters. When, after a while, we jested him about them and, at his request, gave him the written letters, he began to draw these too, and finally was able to do easily what others obtain only after laborious study —that is, he was able to copy and put down whatever he pleased.

How much time both he and I have thus saved! How much more he has been able to enjoy the fresh air! How much more rarely he has been scolded, and how much easier it has been for him to keep his hands, face, and garments clean. If he wants to write caligraphically, he can acquire this art, as I have, in his nineteenth or twentieth year in a period of four weeks, without having wasted much of his previous time.

One important reason why I did not teach him writing in the usual way, was this, that I did not want him to train his attention for writing and then for depending on the written word. This is so frequently done, especially at university lectures, and all it produces is heroes of memory. If such writing machines do not repeat exactly what has been committed to paper, they do not turn out to be even heroes of memory. But my son always paid attention to what was said, and made but the rarest use of notes, hence he was able to master the whole of a lecture, which he soon did to the complete satisfaction of his academic teachers, as well as my own, as their testimonies certify.

I here communicate still another letter game, which we learned later in Wildeck at the court of Hessen-Rothenburg. The players seated themselves about a round table. Upon it were thrown a large mass of letters, ciphers, etc. (about an inch in height and pasted on cardboard). Now each one in the company took a few of them and formed one, two, three, or more syllables with them. Then he mixed them up and gave them to his neighbor. There are five words, he would say. The first begins with k, the second with p, the third with v, the fourth with h, the fifth with r. At the same time the letters were placed vertically below one another, so that the person searching could more easily observe them all and form the words desired. This may lead to an incredible facility. The very beautiful and intellectual Klotilde, Princess of Hessen-Rothenburg, guessed almost anything in a few moments, no matter whether it was German, French, or Italian. The players may tease one another by questions and answers, and a thousand opportunities present themselves for attractively occupying the mind.

All the useful and pleasing games which we learned in Berlin, Leipsic, etc., or else read about, we played with Karl, purposely confusing him, as much as the rule of the game allowed. Very often we arbitrarily modified the game, whenever we saw that it would thus be improved. This is very instructive, because one thus enters into the inner structure of the game, hence passes from the mechanical execution of the rules to a conscious reasoning about them. When Karl later had mastered higher mathematics, it became an easy matter for him to play well every game that was based on calculation, to make changes in such games, or to invent entirely new, and often much more attractive, ones. I must confess, I was perplexed when he made the first attempt at this.

I paid sleight-of-hand men to teach us some of their tricks and to explain others. I thus attained my object, which was that Karl should not only watch the performance, but should also try to find the key to this or that trick himself, in which he frequently was successful. As soon, however, as I noticed that he by his ability in imitation acquired what in the end is a useless art of winning admiration and applause, especially from the fair sex, I avoided such occasions, and, favored by circumstances, I let him forget his tricks and his skill in them. Consequently, the rich spring of bubbling applause ran dry, even as I wished.

CHAPTER XVIII

ON THE SEPARATION OF WORK AND PLAY

ABBÉ GAULTIER is right—one may accomplish an unusual amount with children by means of a sensibly devised and guided game. I differ from him only in this, that I set aside every day a small amount of time for formal instruction, which is not given playfully, though merrily. At first I was moved to do this by my natural instinct. Later I pondered it carefully. Here are the fruits of my reflections:

Since Gaultier has been practicing his method for thirty years, having worked it out in marvelous detail, his pupils should have become not only possessed of much knowledge, but should also have turned out to be men of great and particularly quick mental powers. One should hear in France of a number of superior men, who have come from Gaultier's school, whereas this is not the case. What is the cause of it? I say: The boy who in his early years has learned everything playfully, will continue to wish to learn in that manner. If he cannot do so, he will lose the desire for learning. If he enters business life, where there can be no thought of playing, where he will find everything determined according to order in place, time, and circumstances; where iron necessity demands, now this activity, now that; and where the question is always of work, then he feels out of sorts, hankers for his former playing, and life appears tiresome and annoying to him. He will, consequently, accomplish but little, no matter what may be expected of him.

Therefore I stuck to my method, which was carefully to separate work from play. Each of these had and retained its specific manner. For example, in a game I liked to have Karl put his mental powers to full activity, and we tried to stimulate them, but that was not a requisite. If he did differently, we would perhaps act as though we did not notice it, or we would laugh at him, saying, "Oh, you little goose! is that all you know?" If his answer was not appropriate, not incisive enough, we would again jest him, "You are, indeed, still a very foolish little creature.

One sees that from your answers." He knew then precisely what we meant to convey, and was sure to try to be less foolish and simple.

It was quite different in the case of work. At first I gave him a lesson of but fifteen minutes each day, but during these fifteen minutes he had to collect all his mental powers. I would have become angry if he had not done so. He had to perform everything that was in his power to perform. During work every visit, every inquiry from my wife or the servant was rejected. I said decidedly, "I can't now! We are working!" or "Karl is having his lesson!" My wife and our intimate friends frequently gave me an occasion —out of love for Karl—to pronounce such earnest words with a somewhat gloomy expression and with decided emphasis. The firmness in executing my purpose went so far that even our house-dog knew the emphasis of the words, "I must work!" and calmed down the moment we spoke these words softly into his ears. Almost from the outset this made an enormous impression upon Karl. He soon became accustomed to look upon his work-time as something sacred.

And he had not only to work continuously,

but also with as much vigor and rapidity as he could. I was impatient if he worked slowly, even though he did his work well. This has been of very great use to him; it has given his mind an unusual quickness of perception. Things are often mere trifles to him, though they are very hard for others. He is done, when we only get ready. He thus gains very much time for other matters, for rest, society, and movement in the open, yet he does things better and more thoroughly than we do.

In his later years he came properly to see and honor this invaluable gain. In Vienna he thanked me for it with tender emotion, assuring me that while he had not always understood why I demanded that he should work not only well but also fast, he was now deeply grateful to me for the great advantage he had derived from my insistence.

CHAPTER XIX

CONCERNING REWARDS

WE never rewarded Karl with money or things of value for a good deed. His pure joy at the success of an act; his pleasure at having overcome himself, and our fondling; the noting down of the occurrence in his "Book of Conduct"; the greater attachment of our friends; the firm conviction that God loved him so much the more, and that he now had the power of making one more step in the direction of goodness; finally (wherever it was possible to place them before him) the wholesome consequences of his good deed—that was all his reward. For he was convinced that every good act made him more like God, and his highest wish, his most earnest endeavor, was to become like God.

We acted in the very opposite way in the case of bad acts. Thank Heaven, he did not commit any, but even missteps were by us reproved very earnestly and with an expression of sorrow. We spoke with the greatest contempt of a man, no matter who he may have been, who was the cause of an offense. I am sure that a million dollars could not have moved my son to offend any one knowingly.

But we had no compunction about making a monetary reward for his labors to acquire knowledge. On such occasions we pointed out to him that his efforts would sharpen his wits, but his wits were, in all our conversations, placed far below his heart, especially his spirit of piety. We assured him, and he experienced it in himself, that one could gain men's respect by knowledge and mental powers. But he respected the best more than the many: the love of the best men, of his parents, and of God was worth infinitely more to him than the respect of the masses. He knew also that the latter was unstable, the former stable.

When he had worked hard, we only said, "That is right! You have done your duty, and I am satisfied with you!" and so forth. Then I told his mother or a friend about it in nearly the same words. A good action of his, however, was mentioned to him, to his mother, or to an intimate friend, with a joyous sensation, with a kind of ecstasy, as something sacred. In short, we had him keep in mind that diligent work was a preparation which made one happy in an earthly way, whereas noble actions gave one heavenly satisfaction.

However, I allowed monetary rewards in case of work well done, as a kind of earthly recompense. In this I imitated business life as much as possible. So long as his labors were insignificant, I gave him extremely little, and he knew full well that he had not earned even that little, but that he received it as a visible recognition of his earnest endeavor. Besides, I was careful not to satiate him in matters of rewards. I knew that rewards easily passed into mere payments, and thus lost their higher value. But this was not to happen in the case of Karl.

I am almost ashamed to mention the fact that for a day on which he had read German very well, and had otherwise behaved well, he received only one penny as a reward. But for this very reason I was able in later years, so long as such a direct reward was necessary on account of the boy's shortsightedness, to reward a particularly hard piece of work with a dime. Oh, with what joyous gratitude he used to receive such money! I am sure that many a person is not so happy when receiving dollars!

Wherever it was possible, I kept an ennobled civic life in view. Our family was for him the State, I its regent, and he a servant of state. I demanded of him that for the weal of all, consequently of himself as well, he should exert his whole strength, that is, should do his duty, and should make himself more fit for doing useful work in the future. Consequently all that was written down in his "Book of Conduct" was that he had done what he should, that is, his duty. But I accepted every piece of work done by him diligently and earnestly as something done for my benefit. And so I rewarded it with money. This view could be maintained the more easily since we—the State—provided for him. It was easy afterward for us to give and for him to grasp the more direct instruction of how matters were done in the State, since it followed from my representation.

The money which he collected, on its side, gave an opportunity for preparation for the future. He learned how to manage it and do good with it. If he had spent it on sweetmeats, it would have disappeared very soon, and, with his manner of education, he would not have derived any real pleasure from this. Instead, he saved his money until he had a sufficient amount with which to buy something lastingly useful. This we approved of and we even secretly added enough money to make up the needed amount, and frequently directed his attention to his possessions, to their usefulness and durability. In the end he often made a present of what he had bought to another child, and thus gained the gratitude of children and the love of their parents.

Whenever there was some misfortune in the neighborhood, we helped along according to our means, and we never neglected the three, six, or nine pennies which he offered under such circumstances. On the contrary, we accepted them with "sincere thanks" in the name of the unfortunates, and I sent them to them, even if the case demanded that I should change the pennies into so many dimes. His eight or twelve pennies for the organ stood in my private account close to my twenty dollars, and I explained to him that he had given at least as much as I, referring him to the excellent words of Christ about the poor widow's mite (Mark xii, 42-45), which he had long ago learned from the Biblical stories.

If, however, he had done his very best work but at the same time had transgressed against the laws of a higher morality, he received no money. If the transgression was small, I would say:

"If to-morrow you will be as diligent as to-day, and at the same time will be good, you shall receive to-day's portion also."

He was usually his own severest judge. He never became dissatisfied with the punishment, but rather melancholy at his faulty conduct, at the worry which he thus had caused us, and at the loss of love and respect from the Highest.

Very often he pronounced his own sentence, "No, I cannot get anything to-day, because I did not conduct myself in the proper manner." God knows how hard it was for me then, for example, in the case of very small transgressions, not to give him anything. I would gladly have given him double the amount, and kissed him besides. I bravely repressed the tear of joy, and calmly said to him, "That is so, I did not think of it! But, my boy," and he was kissed none the less, "you must behave better to-morrow!"

By this procedure we accomplished an incredible amount of good. I wish all parents would do likewise for the good of themselves and of their children.

As soon as a larger task was done,—for example, when a book was read through and translated,—he and I would call out in high jubilee, "Long live Gedike, or Jacobs, etc." That was a sign for his mother, who, however, had been secretly informed of it by me before, that there was going to be a celebration.

Such a celebration consisted in this, that his mother prepared one of Karl's favorite dishes, apple pie, waffles with warm beer, or even an omelet with wine sauce, etc., for his supper; that the table was festively set; but especially that his father had a bit of joyous news to tell about Karl's diligence and zeal, about his persistence, his progress, his increased mental powers, the contents of the book just finished and the one to be begun. Thus was the simple supper seasoned. Generally his mother or an intimate friend, who pretended to have dropped in by accident or had been invited by Karl, had the king of the feast tell something from the book just studied, and this gave him much pleasure.

Gratitude toward God for the power and health given us for the work successfully completed was never forgotten on such occasions, and his mother would remind him that he also owed thanks to his teacher for the pains taken with him.

CHAPTER XX

How Karl Learned the Languages

In Karl's sixth year we made a long journey to Berlin and Rostock, and on our way back visited our brother-in-law, Preacher Seide at Stendal. His youngest son, Heinrich, was two years older than Karl, a pretty, lovely boy. His stepmother and her sister, who both loved him tenderly, had taught him so much French that he read and translated very well, and spoke and wrote it tolerably well. That caused me so much pleasure that I warmly expressed my respect and love for the child and for his teachers.

Louise, too, was heartily glad for her nephew, but at the same time was provoked at me, because "Karl did not yet know anything." I laughed at her, and assured her that Karl knew quite a lot, just as all our relatives and friends had asserted in her presence. Of course, he could not know what I had not taught him.

"Why do you not teach him?" she replied.

"You know it, and it is really a shame for us that he is still so ignorant." I reminded her that the time was not yet ripe for it. She retorted, "It will not kill him now, and you cannot tell how long you may live, considering the state of your health. It will certainly take a long time—so why should you be afraid?"

I smiled, and stuck to my idea. But when we went away from Stendal, and I on the way once more mentioned Heinrich with great pleasure, my wife again began to urge upon me. Finally I became annoyed, and said:

"My dear, please do not make my journey unpleasant! I promise you I will teach Karl a foreign language as soon as we are back home. But I tell you I will not give him more than fifteen minutes each day for instruction. I will teach him only to show you that he can learn when he is taught."

"You will not forget, will you?"

"Have I not always kept my word, when I have made a promise?"

We were silent, and I thought of Heinrich and of Karl, and of the manner of the instruction I was going to give.

I busied myself with thinking of this during the rest of our journey. If I had had complete command of Dutch and English (I understood both tolerably well), I should have begun with Plattdeutsch, which Karl to some extent knew already through my wife, through me, and through his frequent travels in northern Germany. Then I would have taken up in turn Dutch, English, French, Italian, Spanish, Latin, and finally Greek.

I should not have been afraid of the near relationship of German, Plattdeutsch, Dutch and English, because the Plattdeutsch is sufficiently differentiated from the German for an intelligent man to keep them easily apart. Karl would be called on to translate English and Dutch into correct German, but not German back into those languages, consequently there would be nothing to fear in the case of a properly instructed boy, while the learning of the languages would be very easy.

I also wish to remark that in theory the Greek language unites many things which make it easy to learn immediately after a thorough knowledge of German has been acquired. Both have the article, decline the nouns, etc., conjugate the verbs, build up the sentence, compound words, and so forth. But who speaks or writes Greek? Where is now the ancient Greece? Have we a Greek children's world? In what way are we to stimulate a child's desire to study Greek, or show him its usefulness? And, finally, although I read Greek with ease and pleasure, I was far better acquainted with French and Italian. And all this is, in teaching languages, of far more importance than most people would be willing to admit.

In the end I chose, after mature reflection, to start by teaching Karl the French language. Here are my reasons for it:

I consider it a duty to teach a child only that with which he has formerly become indirectly acquainted. This was exactly the case with Karl as regards French. I both spoke and read that language. He was frequently in company where I had to speak it. Those with whom I conversed in it he respected and loved on account of their extensive knowledge, but it pained him to listen without being able to tell what they were laughing about. My friends and I generally chose French for intimate conversations. He had also noticed that we were sometimes talking about him. If he later inquired about what had been said, I purposely gave him such answers as only roused his curiosity still more, and then I would add:

"If you only understood French! It would give you much pleasure and gain respect for you."

It is true that a boy who has mastered Latin may with ease pass over to the daughter languages, Italian, French, and so forth. But it is equally true that instruction in Latin before instruction in the foreign languages must appear as something stupid and noisome to a German boy, especially if by that time his spirit has been properly trained. Otherwise, to be sure, he patiently accepts everything like an empty bottle.

They say that he who knows the mother well may easily become acquainted with her daughters. I say to this that he who knows the daughters well will more certainly and more quickly become intimate with their mother. For a younger person it is, besides, easier to make the acquaintance of the daughters before that of the mother.

And to the assertion that he who knows

Latin will find it easier to learn Italian, French, etc., I further answer:

"Very well! If I am on the roof of a building, it is not hard for me to get to the third, second, first story, and finally to the basement. But how shall I get on the roof? It would surely be more sensible—as it is easier and safer—first to enter the basement, then to ascend to the first story, the second, the third, and so forth. In this manner I can finally reach the roof, and that, too, in such an easy way that I scarcely notice it. The difficulty connected with this is as nothing in comparison with the attempt to reach the top from the outside. Besides, I can proceed with less danger, because I proceed in a natural way, and it will hardly take as much time on my way up as on the much praised old way."

When I say to a bright child "pater," he will immediately reply, "That means 'father.' But where is 'the'?" If I say, "It is contained in the word 'pater,'" he will laugh and retort, "That is impossible," or, more likely, "stupid." If, assuming that he already knows the German declensions, he hears that "of the father" is translated by "patris," he will stare at me or become impatient, because it is unthinkable to him that "of the" should be wanting in the declension. It is quite different with the French If I say to my pupil, "'Father' is 'le père,'" he is satisfied, and so he is when he hears that "of the father" is "du père."

But I pass over to the verbs. If I say, "'Ædifico' means 'I build,'" the boy becomes confused and immediately asks, "Where is the 'I'?" But it is perfectly clear to him that "je batis" means "I build." The same is true of "ædificas," "thou buildest," "tu batis," etc. In the plural the Latin appears as a rule still more senseless to children.

This takes place in the case of a bright, or rather well-prepared, boy, for the dull, or unprepared, or improperly prepared boy takes everything in that he is told, especially what is written down in a book—in, for example, the incontrovertible grammar. He goes ahead learning, even the utterly to him incomprehensible "singular, plural, nominative," etc. In fact, he is frightened when he is for the first time asked whether he understands those stock words. And so in after life he will not understand hundreds of things, which he will prejudge in a short-sighted and coarse manner, demanding that others should accept his incorrect view, only because he calls himself learned.

Or, take the past tense, for example, "I have built, ædificavi." The child must feel quite uncomfortable with it. How much more natural it is, "je, I; have, ai; built, bati." So with "Thou hast built," etc. Still more perplexing is the subjunctive. Intelligent children are, in the customary manner of instruction, tormented for a long time by it, without ever gaining a clear insight into it. I marvel how this can even for a moment be doubted. I may add that in the past twenty years a number of bright young men have grasped my idea and that many children have since been taught in accordance with it.

I first searched out that which coincided most closely with the German and rendered it exhaustively into German words. That may generally be accomplished, and the child retains it at once, thinks of it at another juncture, and then translates the words correctly. If some irregularity turned up, I said, for example, "Now that is nice! Here 'dire' does not mean 'tell,' but 'to tell' (that is, in the expression 'pour me dire')." The child does not mind a thing like that, if it recurs regularly, because he has been finding and removing difficulties before. The sentence, "J'ai entendu, qu'on m'a appellé. Est il vrai?" I treated in the following manner. I resolved "j'ai" into "je" and "ai," and jestingly remarked that the French considered "j'ai" as more agreeable to the ear than "je ai," and that they were not entirely wrong in this. After a while Karl began to feel the same way himself, and he took the part of the French. " 'Je ai' or 'j'ai' means 'I have,' and 'entendu' means 'heard.' " It was not necessary to say anything about "qu'on." He may have asked himself, "Is this not the same as in the case of 'je ai'?" and similarly he would say that "m'a" was contracted from "me a." "Me—me, a—has, appellé—called. Est—is, il" (he immediately understood the drawing over of t to est, because it was based on a similar principle) "he, or it." At this point I interposed, "You must find out for yourself which of the two is to be used. All I will tell you for the purpose is that 'vrai' means 'true.'" No sooner had I said this than he answered correctly, "'Il' here means 'it.'"

It will be objected that this is a kind of crippled translation, and that the pupil would thus get used to a poor German. But I can assure the reader from long experience that such is not the case. It may be true to some extent of Latin, because the sentence structure differs too much from that of the German. But it does not hold in the case of French. If, besides, the pupil has become accustomed to speak a pure and fluent German, he will, it is true, at first translate as mentioned above. But as soon as the sentence is finished, he will repeat it in correct German. Let us, however, assume the almost unthinkable case that he would not do so, I should still by far prefer his precise and exhaustive word-for-word translation to giving the sentence in good German, as is usually done, without clearly understanding each word.

"But what will you put in place of analysis?" I am asked. Why, I let Karl first master common sense and the German language, derive, decline, transpose, and substitute the separate words, etc., and exercise his reason.

After that the translation from a foreign language was treated precisely like the reading of a German author. The main point was that Karl should get the exact meaning of the passage. If, therefore, a word or phrase was not clear to him, he thought it over or asked us. If he failed to do so, we asked him. In short, he became accustomed to the desire to understand everything. With the above-mentioned method he was never in the dark, for it is a boon to a boy brought up in this manner to get an account of the various cases in which a word may occur. He considers it a great kindness to have it looked up for him in the grammar, have it read to him, or pointed out where in the future he may find words similarly declined.

Hence, whenever Karl was translating, the dictionary lay to the right, and the grammar to the left of him. For the same reason, I prefer for a beginner such readers as have small dictionaries attached to them, for the looking up of words in the large dictionary may still be too troublesome and confusing. Some readers have also a small grammar connected with them, but I have made no use of these, because a child should from the start become accustomed to the grammar which he is to use later. Habit is of extreme importance here, and the finding of the particular references may be made easy by marks stuck between the leaves, thus making extracts from them unnecessary.

Karl never translated without having an exhaustive idea of every expression and without being ready to render it into German. He was, therefore, all the time deeply concerned in knowing how the troublesome word was declined, whether it was in the singular or in the plural, whether a noun or adjective, whether masculine or feminine, etc.

One will observe that he, too, analyzed, but (1) he himself had the desire to do so, and this is, as in all instruction, the important point; (2) he analyzed for a particular purpose, and that was, in order to grasp the context completely. Consequently he was never satisfied until he found out, at first with my aid, later by himself, everything which would clear up his doubts. At the same time he paid attention to everything that stood in close relation with the particular case, and, since he was used to regularity, clearness, etc., he was sure not to look anything up in the dictionary or grammar without purposely noticing many other things connected with it, thus exercising his memory and reason; (3) he analyzed sensibly, with a clear consciousness of what he was doing. Manifestly such an investigation of the words in a sentence is infinitely more useful than the usual mode of analyzing.

I frequently said, with due consideration, "If you want to know this precisely, you will do well to look it up in the grammar, in the dictionary, etc.," and thus I led him deeper into the subject than he had anticipated.

But there are other important reasons why I purposely taught him French before Latin. In French we are dealing with the present world, instead of one dead for millenniums and therefore foreign to the child. The little reader finds in his book our customs, our habits, our climate, our buildings, rooms, utensils, our society, our culture, our social intercourse, our garments, our entertainments, amusements, and so forth. He consequently always feels at home, whereas Rome and Greece, especially with the usual method of instruction, remain an alien and less attractive world to him. Nearly all the incidents in an author of modern times seem to have happened in the boy's vicinity, while stories from ancient Rome and Greece all the time remind him forcibly of the great difference between their world and his surroundings. This in itself would be sufficient to characterize the instruction which begins with Latin and Greek as putting the cart before the horse. But my main reason is still to come.

I am indeed convinced that a child will be glad to learn reading any language, and will acquire it profitably, only if he is given easily understood writings, best of all such as have been written with care for children. The child is to find in them a children's world, if possible. The arena, the actions, and the persons should be childlike (not childish), and we in Germany are particularly fortunate in possessing many excellent books of the kind. The French and the English, even the Italians, have for this reason translated the better German books for children, although they are wary in translating our other literary works. We rejoice in this advantage, and we make use of it in our language. Should we not do the same in a foreign, that is, a more difficult, language? Should we here purposely push the children's world aside, and lead our darlings upon a desert steppe that for them is filled with thorns and thistles? I cannot be a party to it, for they will wander about disheartened in it, and they will bring back few fruits.

But give them funny little stories from their circle, such as are found in a well-prepared reader, and all those who have received the right kind of an education will eagerly learn the language in which they are written. They will gladly make the necessary efforts of mind and memory, and will quickly and easily overcome obstacles, because their work gives them pleasure. It will not take long before they will of their own accord read beyond the task set them, and you will attain what you wish to attain, if you are sensible. All that is needed besides is an intelligent guidance, and the children attain to higher perfection by themselves.

I gave Karl as quickly as possible Berquin's "Ami des Enfants," which can be bought very cheaply of Grieshammer at Leipsic. He read, I believe, through eighteen numbers of it, in high glee, and rejoiced especially whenever he there found the translation of a German juvenile story with which he was already acquainted. He would read ten pages of it without being asked to do so, and soon learned so much from it that I had to pass to more difficult writings. He was attracted by the childlike, droll, witty material, drawn from his circle, that was so simple for comprehension and appealed to his reason and heart. This made his none too hard labor pleasant for him.

It would have been quite another thing, if I had begun with Latin and had at once given him Cornelius Nepos, as generally happens. I will mention only a few of the resultant difficulties, as compared with Berquin. The language of Nepos has long been dead. No man speaks it. It is not native to any country. Hence the child foresees no reward for his efforts, and yet any child, no matter how unreasoning it may be, must always have that clearly placed before its eyes. Besides, that language has no article; it declines and conjugates differently from our language; it places the words in the sentence so differently, so bluntly, and often with such intricacy that even grown persons find it hard to make out the sense.

All that refers only to the external side. The internal side is much worse off. Books such as I require are made for children. Cornelius Nepos, Julius Cæsar, Cicero, and so forth, wrote for men, for republicans, hence for statesmen, and for men who lived two thousand years ago. Cornelius, more especially, wrote for grown-up Romans, who ruled over Greece, partly studied there, and therefore were more or less acquainted with Greek language, literature, and manners. He wanted to be helpful to them by a terse and succinct account of the deeds of great Greek generals and their campaigns, for they needed mere hints as to names, places, time, and so forth. It did not harm them when he mentioned vices of every kind, even the most unnatural, without any sense of shame. According to their code of morals, their religion, it was permissible, or at least excusable, if Alcibiades honorably distinguished himself among the Persians and Thracians as a debauchee and winebibber.

But what impression will all that produce on an innocent, Christian child? What is such a little creature to do with the masterpiece of military tactics which Cæsar, under special circumstances, invented anew or modified, and which he described, indeed, in a masterly way, but one which is almost too much abbreviated even for an advanced warrior? What is he to do with the legal and political writings of Cicero? Or with his Græco-Roman philosophical works, by which he wanted to win the best men of Rome over to the most profound investigations of Greece? Of what good to a boy of ours are Cicero's letters to his "intimate" friends, since Cicero all the time takes for granted much they very well knew, but which our boys neither guess at, nor want to guess at, and of which nine-tenths of their teachers know precious little? If a boy has painfully plowed his way through Cornelius, even as I did, what has he gained from it? I know but few useful results from it, and a great mass of harmful ones.

On the other hand, how rich the gain is for the intellect, imagination, wit, and heart if the boy has attentively read and finished a German or French book appropriately written for German or French children! I am sure I shall be wasting time and labor and undervaluing my readers' intelligence if I say anything more about this. I will only add that I consider it a sin against our intelligence and that of our children, to begin with the philosophy of language, that is, with grammar, and to treat only incidentally, or allow to follow later, the language treasure, that is, the very subject which is to be judged and regulated. I proceeded in the reverse order, and that did my son a great deal of good.

But, it will be remarked, "The reading of French is so very difficult, whereas the reading of Latin is easy." That is true—a proof that objections may be raised against anything. But it did not bother me, when I wanted to instruct Karl, and Karl wanted to be instructed. I at first gave him such words as were pronounced as with us, then such as differed a little, and so forth.

At the same time I united earnest with jest. Earnest—for I taught him at once the correct pronunciation of the French letters, and showed him a mass of cases where it actually was used. Jest—because even in the case of the German words which are written irregularly, I had frequently said, "This shows how silly we still are, for, instead of writing 'tuhn,' we write 'thun,' and so forth. The French are even sillier in writing, or, rather, in the pronunciation of what they have written." So he looked upon it as being funny, and it even gave him pleasure to busy himself with the senseless stuff, because he treated it, now as a trick, now as a puzzle, now as a maze, in dealing with which he had to bring light and clearness. I aver as an honest man that in this way he learned French with incredible rapidity. What differed most from the norm was mentioned to him with the greatest ridicule, and, upon occasion, in a farcical manner; or he was reminded of it at table or during a walk, by saying, for example, "Oh, this is almost as sensible as the French pronunciation of 'monsieur'!"

I should like to mention here in general that our children would learn a great deal more if we looked less imposing during our lectures. I am opposed to the method of teaching wholly through play, yet I consider it necessary to combine jest with earnestness. My beloved and honored teacher, Gedike, always did so.

Karl frequently learned difficult things easily, because I offered them to him in a merry and a light way, while slight difficulties frightened him if I or some one else assumed an official mien, or presented the subject in a cold, stiff, anxious, indistinct, or confused manner.

What is bad, I might say what is abominable, is that much is taught which the teacher himself does not master. Just as most German actors do not know their parts well, hence anxiously look and listen to the prompter and speak in long-drawn-out and incorrect passages, not thinking of the correct expression, proper action, and easy playing, and thus annoying and tiring out the spectator; so do the teachers fail in their purpose who do not master the subject of instruction, do not know it from all sides, do not present it lightly to the child. Instead of joy the hearer will experience a sense of burden, instead of active participation, ennui and disgust. He who teaches children, stopping to think about his subject, or sticking to what has just been read, or frequently looking into the text-book, will not be able to impart much to them. I have experienced this in my own case and in the case of others, at first as a pupil, and later as a teacher, but fortunately I have had also the opposite before my eyes. For this reason I taught my son only what I could in the highest degree call my own mental property.

If I had wanted to hurry, I should have given Karl an hour's instruction each day, instead of fifteen minutes, or should have had recourse to the conversational method. But I was afraid of prematurity and did only what I had to, at Louise's request. In a few months I joyfully observed that the child was gaining and wanted to study more; so I gave him half an hour, after a while a little more, and toward the end of the year an hour each day. Karl got only pleasant things for his reading. He was given, for example, "Robinson Crusoe," which he knew already from the German, and which he later translated from nearly all the languages. In a year he was so far advanced that he could with pleasure read an easy French book without my aid. I then began speaking French with him, and passed on to the study of Italian. This was so easy for him that he made as much progress in it in six months as he had made in French in a year. The longest study period now lasted an hour and a half.

Karl had learned to know and to overcome

any peculiar difficulties which had occurred in either language. So I hoped that he would no longer be afraid of Latin. I should have hoped not in vain, but a large number of grown persons and of his young friends, especially two pupils at my house, had frequently spoken to him of Latin as something extremely disagreeable, difficult, and useless, and so he had an anxiety and prejudice against it.

I was not able to remove these, since, from what I said above, I could not promise him either ease or great pleasure. Nor did I see clearly how I could make its usefulness manifest to him as in the case of the modern languages. To have assured him that he could become a learned man only through the knowledge of Latin would have been of no avail, for he could have answered rightfully that he did not care to become a learned man, but rather a well-rounded, cultured man, which he certainly might do without Latin. He had several examples of this kind before his eyes, and uncountable examples of learned men without true culture of mind or heart. There was, therefore, nothing left for me to do but to assure him, upon good faith and through my nearest friends, that the study of

Latin was important and necessary. I also frequently spoke in his presence of the beauties of the Æneid and of separate works of Cicero. For what honest man, who is not a self-satisfied scholar, can recommend to his son the works of Ovid, Terence, Suetonius, Horace, and so many other Latin and Greek classics, without trembling for his morality? Only a learned "æs triplex circa pectus" can assuage conscience, if the boy should become a drunkard, a debauchee, or given to unnatural vices, for have not the most shameful incitements toward it, and the most violent stimuli for his passions, been given into his hands as something extremely praiseworthy?

Accordingly, when Karl had command of his Latin, I did something quite unusual. I used to speak of some author, for example Horace, with high respect as a poet, man of the world, and philosopher, and with the utmost contempt as a drunkard and debauchee. I never said in such a case that he drank, but that he was a drunkard, a sot. For expressions such as "to appropriate" for "to steal," "not to tell the truth" for "to lie," "not industrious" for "lazy," do an incredible amount of harm in common life, and much more in education. Vice is most dangerous in an attractive garment. My judgments of the authors had a good effect on Karl, though they might have been harmful in the case of hundreds of other boys. He had faith in me and judged like me, for he respected and loved me devotedly. Besides, he had been accustomed not to want to read a thing if I said, "It is not good for you!" but especially if my face indicated contempt or disgust. Children brought up in the ordinary way strive so much the more to read what is prohibited, or to talk about it with others. Unfortunately such passages are, as a rule, the only ones which are appropriated by them to the full extent.

Yet, in spite of all I have said above, I could not overcome my misgivings, and so I chose an edition of Horace which at that time was expurgated as regards the vilest matter, and I liked it well. Of course, there were not wanting those who asserted that in that way he could not become a great Latin scholar, and that those passages did less harm than usually supposed, and so forth. I listened to their balderdash and pitied their pupils, since their innocent minds could not help being ruined by those shameless atrocities.

I mentioned above why I could not recommend Cæsar to Karl. Livy is for a child too earnest, too dry. Especially his introduction is much too difficult. I should have chosen the fables of Phædrus least of all, because I myself had to suffer the torture of beginning with them.

A happy circumstance helped me out of my perplexity as to how to lead Karl over to Latin. I was frequently at Leipsic with Karl, attending the theater, the concert, in short, everything worth seeing. Once they played the "Stabat Mater," and at the entrance they gave me the text for it. Karl had been accustomed to having the contents of this kind read or translated to him. During the symphony we were sitting in a side-room, and I said to him, "Do translate this!" He took it, then looked for a moment perplexedly at it, and said, "This is neither French nor Italian. It must be Latin." I replied, laughing, "Let it be what it may, if only you can translate it. Try at least!" He tried, and I helped him, especially by pronouncing the harsh Latin sounds somewhat softer, almost like Italian, for example, "stava't," "mader," "dolorosa," etc. Coming to words like "juxta," I helped him out by saying, "You do not know this, it means so and so." "Crucem" I pronounced as in Italian; the *c* in "lacrimosa" almost like *g*, and so forth. In fine, we translated it with fair rapidity and merrily to the very end. He said, with joy, "If that is all there is to it, I should like to learn Latin!" "Of course, that is all, and, in case of need, I can help you out." The very next day I hunted up the Latin "Robinson" and other easy readers which are appropriate for children.

I began with these, caring precious little whether the language was Ciceronian or not.[1] It took nine months before Karl had accomplished as much in Latin as he had in Italian in six months, although the two daughter languages, which he had already acquired, had

[1] Of course, one should not choose the "Epistolæ Obscurorum Virorum" or give children similar books Most important of all is it to bear in mind that a child may best be led to a complete comprehension of the Latin classics by beginning with a good translation of German juvenile books, and it will be accomplished much more rapidly, because the child likes to read them and out of curiosity will frequently read ahead of the daily task At the same time his intellect is kept immeasurably more active; his knowledge is greatly increased and rectified; and, what is most important, his heart remains pure and may even be ennobled. Then one may pass over to the Æneid, to some of the more attractive writings of Cicero, and to a few other, morally pure or, at least, purified classics, and the child will learn his Latin fast enough.

prepared the way to a very considerable extent. A number of deviations from the German were already known to him, and they seemed natural to him. Other deviations he did not mind, because he had been brought by degrees to these, for a German child, unnatural forms.

At the end of the time mentioned I lived with him for six weeks at my quarters in Halle, staying there for several days each week, and I employed the services of an expert teacher of languages for the pronunciation of English. During the hour Karl studied together with me. After it we repeated the old and prepared the new lesson together. English now became so easy to him that he understood as much of it in three months as of the others in six or nine month

How difficult, however, the Greek language is for a German child, I found in my own case, in the case of numberless friends, and especially in that of Karl. He wanted to learn it; I had told him so much about Homer, Xenophon, Plutarch, and most of all about a mass of lovely flowers from the Greek world which are collected in our best readers, that he was anxious to acquire them. Yet, although Greek is an elder sister of German, the two sisters have, through time and circumstances, developed such different idioms that it is very difficult for a German child to learn Greek. "Græca sunt, nec leguntur" has become especially clear to me since my last experience.

Even before beginning Greek with Karl, I had given him, at his urgent request, two or three months' instruction in it in secret—that is, from his mother and other friends—each lesson lasting fifteen minutes, and he had worked hard at it. I then somewhat increased the lessons, to please him, or I gave him an additional lesson of fifteen minutes, say, in the evening, when he asked for it in particular. And yet, after three months, he was discouraged and thought he would never learn it, and it took him nine months to be as far in Greek as he had been in the other languages in a shorter time. But, as soon as these first difficulties were overcome, he made very good progress.

I think I can hear two objections. First, people will say, "How many hours did you use, to keep all the languages mentioned going? The child must have been sitting all day at the desk, hence he must have become stupefied!" Experience has shown the reverse, and, with my method of instruction, must prove it absolutely. But these people are absolutely right, if they have in mind that which is taking place at present. If I had begun with Latin or Greek, or if I had not carefully prepared the child's intellect; if I had neglected to teach Karl to speak excellent German in the first five years of his life; if I had not roused his love for the foreign languages in many ways, and had not laid their great usefulness clearly before his eyes; if I had not gotten him used to work rapidly, while sparing him from those abominable "versions" which take away hours at a time and accustom a boy to dilly-dallying; the instruction in four or five languages all at once would have been a sheer impossibility, if for nothing else than lack of time.

As it was, everything went excellently. The moment Karl had brushed aside the chief difficulties, I gave him only fifteen minutes a day in which, for example, to continue his French. During that period he had to read for himself a considerable passage, looking up everything he did not know in the dictionary and grammar, in order to give me an exhaustive account of it in German. At the end of his study period I would quiz him here and there. I generally knew where to look for the difficulties—and then I had him recite to me, now literally, now in choice German. If two such passages went off well, I considered his work done well in every way. It is incredible what rapidity, besides precision, a boy may gain by this way of working. He is kept mentally busy, and so advances with all due speed. The mechanical writing retards him, causes him ennui, and tires him even of the most attractive passage. Try both methods for any length of time,—but do it honestly—and then pass judgment!

Besides, while out walking, traveling, etc., we at first conversed frequently in French, later in Italian, and finally also in Latin or English. One may see that a boy, if he is willing, may in this manner accomplish very much by employing at most three hours each day. Karl did not receive more instruction than that in Lochau, that is, up to his tenth year. Indeed, if I take into consideration the Sundays, the frequent travels, etc., he did not have more than two hours each day of actual instruction, before we went to Goettingen. But we frequently read together, or he by himself, in the long winter evenings, or in the afternoon of a rainy day, now a German book for children, now some select passages from foreign languages, which he (more rarely I) had found and wanted to read, or we recited some especially fine poems to one another.

Second objection: "Your son must have confused the various languages." Since the great schoolman, noble Funk of Magdeburg, expressed the same fear, I am not surprised when others do so. But Funk, like many others, became convinced of the contrary, hence I do not need to prove that it is possible or has been accomplished, but need only to tell how it was done. This, of course, goes once more back to Karl's earliest years. Karl had to do everything correctly, had especially to speak good German, was not allowed, except in actual necessity, to introduce foreign words, and so forth. I demanded the same of him in his translations. I admitted nothing but pure German, absolutely nothing else. Besides, he had to be perfectly at home in a language before I began the next. That is all I did, and even envy has not been able to find any fault with his translations, while our greatest philologists have praised him highly, both orally and in writing.

I wish once more to decry that disastrous blunder people make who assert that without beginning with grammar, without that senseless analyzing and without written exercises, it is not possible to learn to speak and write perfect Latin. I had so much facility in both, that Gedike was perfectly satisfied with me, and yet I never did any of those things. But I had read so much the more in the two languages and made their contents my own. If, however, I should have started by teaching my son to speak and write "elegant" Latin, I do not believe I could have attained my purpose without crippling his intellect.

CHAPTER XXI

Karl's Education in the Sciences

It seems ridiculous to talk of this, for Karl could not receive any formal instruction in the sciences at Lochau. In the first place, this belongs to the university, and in the second, a preacher in the country lacks the necessary means for it. I had the required information, or I could get it out of books, but not the mass of newer works, the necessary etchings, the costly instruments, the facility in experimentation, etc. I was, therefore, glad to forego it, but I none the less directed Karl's attention to a mass of scientific facts, without saying to him, "This belongs to natural history, this to chemistry, this to physics, to ancient, or to modern geography, and so forth."

He became acquainted with natural history in all its parts the moment he could think. The much improved edition of Raff was one of his playthings, and in Halle, Leipsic, and

Merseburg he never failed to see the strange animals or anything else worth seeing But most of all I used our travels for this purpose. The sea with its inhabitants, mines and shafts, smelters, steam-engines, air-pumps, a basalt mine, crater-like hollows on the tops of mountains, everything gave me an opportunity for instruction. Even at home, a dewdrop, my barometer, the thermometer, the noisy draught in firing a stove, the sweat on the window-panes, etc.,—how much there is to tell a child about these and about hundreds of similar phenomena, if one has studied with any profit natural history, physics, and chemistry.

I began my instruction in geography in the following manner: I took Karl as soon as possible to all the villages which lay within the horizon of our tower. He was also taken often to Halle, Merseburg, Leipsic, etc. In clear weather I used to ascend the tower with him, taking with me a few sheets of white paper and a pencil. At first we drew (Karl did it more than I) the approximate contour of our village in the middle of the sheet, on an appropriately small scale, so that the rest would fit into the sheet. Then we put down a dot for the nearest village, Liebenau, and so forth for the other visible villages on every side. We at the same time wrote down their names. The rivers Saale and Elster, the forests, meadows, and fields were indicated upon it in red.

When this was done, we showed it to his mother, and she made her remarks upon it. Then we went a second time to the tower, and made a good drawing of the map, which, for us at least, was sufficiently correct. Then we compared it with special maps of the Saale District, and corrected it in the light of the latter. That was all I did in order to give Karl a correct idea of geography, and to rouse his inclination toward it. He never afterward returned from a journey but that he was able to give and indicate upon paper the approximate distances of the places. When he was nine years old, he owned a collection of maps such as I have seldom seen in the possession of wealthy young men. We bought as many of them as we could, and many were given to him as presents.

He had, besides, the maps of d'Anville, and he never read anything from ancient history but that he had them near at hand. I introduced him to history during our walks or upon our journeys, by stories, and employed for the same purpose historical paintings, etchings, etc. Mr. K. v. S. at Merseburg taught him a great deal of astronomy, by means of his excellent instruments. I had previously done all that could be done without a telescope. He was really quite advanced in these things when he was nine years old, but he would have been greatly surprised if he had been told that he had been studying geography, physics, and so forth.

I had carefully avoided the use of such terms, partly in order not to frighten him, partly not to make him vain. He learned them and all other technical terms quickly enough, after he mastered that which they meant. It was with these as with plural, nominative, subjunctive, etc. I did as though he was not to learn them, but as soon as the things were his, the names followed easily.

CHAPTER XXII

THE CULTIVATION OF TASTE

I TOLERATED as far as possible nothing in my house, yard, garden, etc., that was not tasteful, especially nothing that did not harmonize with its surroundings. If anything was not harmonious, I was uneasy about it until it was removed. All my rooms were papered with wall-paper of one color, the fields being surrounded by pleasing borders. In every room there was but little furniture, but such as there was was carefully selected. On all the walls hung paintings or etchings, but none of these was tastelessly glaring in colors, or represented an unpleasant subject. Our yard and garden were in bloom from earliest spring to very late in the fall. Snowbells and crocuses started the procession, and winter asters were only crushed by the snow or a severe frost. We ourselves were always dressed cleanly but simply.

I never bought anything that was too magnificent for my circumstances, nor any pictures for Karl unless they were true and beautiful. If he was presented with a picture which did not come up to the mark, we inspected it jestingly and made fun of what was not beautiful, especially of anything with glaring colors. On the other hand, we frequently admired the color schemes of flowers and birds. But if these were too brightly colored, we did not fail to remark upon it.

Wherever we could obtain anything beautiful, we were sure to do so. Leipsic, Dessau, Woerlitz, Potsdam, Berlin, Rostock, Weimar, Dresden, the Saxon Switzerland, and so forth, furnished me opportunities enough to widen and correct Karl's conceptions of the beautiful. Leipsic and its fair! How much these few words mean! But Karl had known the two very well since early childhood. He had become acquainted with the beauties of Potsdam and Berlin in his fifth year, and of Dresden and its magnificent surroundings when he was only six years old. We visited the picture gallery there for days and weeks in succession, while Mengs's casts and the antiques were visited as often as possible, and the Green Vault twice. We never beheld men, horses, dogs, birds, houses, carriages, furniture, pictures, etc., but that we directed each other's attention to them and discussed them favorably or unfavorably.

Karl learned very early to love and properly to judge poetry. We began with the simplest poems and by degrees rose to the most sublime. The versification, rhyme, language, contents, gentle hints or allusions in these formed the subject of our common judgment. The most beautiful of these Karl learned by heart very rapidly, if we recited them to him a few times on our walks or journeys.

What was the case with German, soon also happened with French, and I aver that in all the languages which he learned he soon knew a mass of excellent poems by heart, because he read them several times for their beauty and thus retained them in his mind. I shall only mention Florian, Metastasio, Virgil, Horace, and Homer. Many a time, when I was particularly busy, he tortured me by reading or reciting to me long passages from the most beautiful poems. But I listened patiently, in order not to spoil his pleasure. Heyne would not have written to Wieland the way he did, if Karl had not even then tried to penetrate the spirit of the ancients.

CHAPTER XXIII

Karl Goes to College

Karl was now seven and a half years old, and his attainments appeared very striking to men of knowledge. One man told another about it. People wanted to examine him, and I allowed this to be done. The above-mentioned K. v. S. in Merseburg was among these, and he soon became Karl's fatherly friend. He did everything he could, with touching zeal, to instruct Karl, for that meant giving him pleasure. He did not value even the rarest wines of his cellar too highly, to let Karl taste of them, in order that he might get an idea of what they were like. His superb library, etchings, instruments,—all these Karl could use as his own. Every time we two had to pass the night with him, on account of astronomical observations, he invited highly cultured men to his house. Thus several schoolmen became acquainted with Karl.

One of these, Mr. T. L., asked permission

to examine him before his students, in order to stimulate the latter. I hesitated for a long time, but finally I consented under the following conditions: (1) Karl was to know nothing in advance of the examination; hence (2) L. was to come for me the following day, under the pretext that I should pass judgment on his pupils, and Karl was then to come with me; (3) the pupils were not to express their approbation; (4) we would sit down on a back bench and listen. Then a book might be handed to us, and so forth. All that was promised, and kept to the letter.

A few weeks later there appeared in the *Hamburger Korrespondent* the following announcement. It was decisive for my son's whole later career, and so it is of great importance for every thinking man. The writer has never become known, but I believe that the noble man will surely be rewarded in a better world for his beautiful purpose.

MERSEBURG, *May* 10, 1808.

A few days ago there happened here something very remarkable for pedagogy. The excellent teacher of our place, Mr. Tertius Landvogt, brought to the schoolroom, for the stimulation of his pupils, a small child of seven years and ten months. The little fellow listened attentively to the Greek lesson which was being recited; then Mr. T. L., who had met him the day before at the house of the very humane and cultured Kammerherr, Mr. von Seckendorf, and had examined his powers in the presence of several scholarly men, asked him to continue the reading. To the astonishment of all the pupils he read and translated a perfectly strange passage from Plutarch, and answered several analytical questions to entire satisfaction.

Now he was given Julius Cæsar, and he translated from the passage where the pupils had stopped. He was also tested in analysis on the passage read and answered the questions very well. Then he translated from an unknown Italian book, which Mr. T. L. had brought, and conversed with his father in this language. Since there was no French at hand, Mr. T. L. spoke French with him, and he answered as fast is if it were German. Then he noticed on the wall a map of ancient Greece, and he asked permission to be allowed to look at it. Then he mentioned the chief cities and countries of Greece, and told about them and about several of their great men. When Sinope was mentioned, he said at once, "That is not here. We must look for it over there, on Pontus Euxinus," pointing to another map on another wall. The pupils carried the child there, and he showed them at once Sinope and told about Diogenes. He mentioned still more cities and countries, and at the same time gave their modern names. Finally he calculated a few problems in the rule of three without the use of paper.

The main thing with all this is the vigorous health and vivacity, the tender, childlike manner and modesty of the boy, who does not seem to know how much he is the object of common admiration.

His father is Preacher Dr. Karl Witte, of Lochau,

well known in educational circles. Unfortunately Dr. Witte does not expatiate on his method of instruction, by which this prodigy, who widely differs from those of Heineke and Baratier, who were spoilt, partly in body and partly in mind, has been brought up and educated in such an indescribably fortunate manner.

This news soon spread in all newspapers. Everybody read it, everybody asked, "Is it true? Can it be true?" Many doubters came to see me, others invited me to their houses. They all examined Karl suspiciously. But everybody left us with the conviction that the boy could do even more than the newspapers had told about him. Only jealous people near by and far away passed judgments, without even wishing to see him, to the effect that it was not true, because it could not be true. Such people usually wait until they find out which way the wind is blowing. In this way they are always swimming on top, and they have the advantage that no one can deny what they finally admit. God save us from such narrow-minded educators! They would like to suppress what is unusual, and would furnish us clever rather than noble-minded pupils. But men who do not merely skim off from the top of what is furnished to them, but enter into matters with their own minds, acted quite differently. They not infrequently wrote to me and asked to have the child shown to them, and I never refused such a request.

Some of the best men of the city and the university of Leipsic urged me to have my son examined for the university by the Rector of the Thomas School, Professor Rost. As I did not know the man, I was afraid that he would consider this step a bit of presumption, and so forth. So I flatly refused, saying that a large number of professors had already examined my son. Finally I yielded. Professor Rost unites great learning with much sound sense and kindness of heart. He introduced my son into the arcana of the languages and sciences, while he thought that he was merely having a pleasant conversation. Here is his testimony:

This day they brought before me the nine-year-old boy, J. H. F. Karl Witte, from Lochau, in order that I might examine him and pass on his intellect and information. I put before him by no means easy passages from the Iliad, the Æneid, Guarini's "Pastor Fido," and a French work, from which he translated so well that he completely justified the continuous assurances of men who are capable of passing judgment, as well as the common reputation of his skill. For in the translation of the passages chosen by me at random, he not only showed a great skill in the verbal knowledge of the various languages, but he also evinced a deep insight into the science of antiquity, a maturity of judgment, a self-possession, and a superior power of all the other mental faculties, such as I have never before seen in so youthful a being. I, therefore, am firmly convinced that the superior aptitudes of the boy and the most excellent educational method of his father, who has trained his son all by himself, deserve the attention of scholars, who should carefully investigate and weigh these matters. I am convinced that it is very necessary, for the good of the sciences in general, and for the advancement of pedagogy in particular, to give this boy of extraordinary mind, who is born for everything great, permission to attend all the lectures of the professors, for which he is unquestionably prepared; and that no hindrance through prejudice should be placed in his way, lest the hope of everything good for which God seems to have prepared him, should be crushed.

MAG. F. W. E. ROST,
Professor of Philosophy and Rector of the Thomas School

LEIPSIC, *December* 12, 1809.

Professor Rost's statement was sent to the University of Leipsic, where consent was given for his admission as a regular student. This took place on January 18, 1810, through the then Rector of the university, Mr. Kuehn. His excellent speech to Karl and me touched us both very much. I was particularly moved when the child gave a handshake, in place of the usual oath, that he would promptly keep the laws. After that Karl received his matriculation. Hereupon the University of Leipsic made an appeal to benevolent wealthy men, to secure my stay in Leipsic fot at least three years, so that my son should be able to attend the lectures, for which he had been found, upon a strict examination, fully mature and capable. Here is the appeal:

The youthful, nine-year-old Karl Witte, son of Dr. Witte, Pastor at Lochau, represents to us a remarkable example of the fact that by a proper early education the mental powers of a child may be trained and brought to an almost incredible degree of maturity, and his memory may be furnished with an amount and variety of information in the first decade of his life, that would do honor to a youth of eighteen. This remarkable child has been translating, not at all mechanically, but with insight, facility, and deep sentiment, both the prose and the poetical writers, in French, Italian, English, Latin and Greek, and of this he has lately given astonishing proofs in the presence of the greatest experts, and also in the presence of His Majesty the King of Saxony, as well as the whole court. He showed a remarkably quick and well-guided comprehension, as well as an uncommon reading in history, the antiquities, ancient and modern geography, and the best poets. All this he owes entirely to his father, who until now has been his only teacher, and whose happy and properly employed gift of instruction is no less remarkable than the early education of his son.

What withal removes the very shadow of a suspicion that all this is the work of an injurious and destructive effort of the child, is his health and childlike merriment, and the complete absence of any of the forwardness and intolerable arrogance displayed by wrongly educated youthful prodigies. His father, who, in conjunction with his excellent wife, has brought the child so early to this degree of knowledge, has the very natural and just desire of further educating him under his own guidance in a manner proportionate to his already acquired information; and there can be no doubt that if the child is further educated under the happy method and surveillance of his father, there should result therefrom something unique and great, and without injury to the child's life and health.

In the simple village, where the family now lives, it is, on account of the father's meager income, impossible to obtain the appropriate instruction in those branches of knowledge which the father does not himself master. It is, therefore, the father's sincerest wish to continue his son in some large city on the path on which he has been started, for at least three more years and under his personal supervision. Nor can it be doubted that he, the loving father of his only son, who has done so much for his child in four years without the least injury to him, will also be able to use to good advantage the three years to come. But the manner in which this is to be accomplished can naturally not be determined by the views and prescriptions of those who have no conception of the natural, as well as pure and thorough, educational method of Dr. Witte.

Dr. Witte needs for the execution of his plan the

assured sum of at least two hundred and fifty dollars a year for the period of three years. If these two hundred and fifty dollars could be guaranteed, his parents would for three years stay in Leipsic, while his father's parish would meanwhile be administered and kept for him by somebody else, or he would be promised another, more profitable one by the royal Westphalian Government. He could use his stay in Leipsic, outside of instructing his son, partly for literary labors, partly and more especially for the instruction of other people's children, perhaps incidentally in order to instruct future educators in his method; hence he could even in this incidental way multiply the usefulness of his stay here.

The question is now whether our fellow-citizens will remain indifferent and inactive lookers-on of this phenomenon, and will be willing to bear the accusation that they have knowingly neglected the cultivation of such a rare plant.

In the firm conviction that such a thing is unthinkable in the case of the noble inhabitants of Leipsic, we herewith invite those whom Providence has placed in a position to further such a beautiful work, to assure by subscription the sum of at least two hundred and fifty dollars for three years to young Witte, for this is the only condition under which his parents can properly continue their work here in Leipsic. Since the boy is now able, of course accompanied by his father, to attend profitably several academic lectures, the university has to-day granted the young Witte the right of academic citizenship, for which, after a strict examination, he was found entirely mature and capable.

Karl Gottlob Kuehn,
Rector of the University.

Leipsic, *January* 18, 1810

Instead of two hundred and fifty dollars the generous people of Leipsic soon subscribed five hundred, besides offering me free quarters and two stipends, not counting what the King was going to do. The condition was that we should stay in Leipsic. I went with Karl to Kassel, in order to obtain there the necessary consent. But the King was not there. The next morning I called on Mr. von Leist. He had great prejudices against me and my son, but soon became fond of him. He examined him for three hours, and marveled at his knowledge, and asked me about my method of instruction. Above all he decided that the boy should not go to Leipsic, but should stay in the country. Then he invited us to dinner for the next day, and invited the ministers and councilors of state then present in Kassel, to examine Karl a few hours before. Both the Germans and the French were highly satisfied, and, after holding council, decided unanimously that the King should supply me with what Leipsic had promised, and that I should with my son go to attend the university at Halle or Goettingen. I flatly refused to go to Halle, and did not even agree to Goettingen. Upon my return to Lochau I found the following ministerial writing:

KASSEL, *July* 29, 1810.

MY PASTOR:

I reported to his Majesty the King about the extraordinary talents and progress of your son, as also about your wish to devote yourself entirely to his education. His Majesty, always graciously inclined to encourage talents, has granted your request to give up your present situation at Michaelmas, and has ordered me to provide another place for you at the expiration of your son's education.

Considering the excellent institutions of learning in the Kingdom, His Majesty wishes that your son's education be finished within the realm, and, for the purpose of indemnifying you for any other possible offers, grants your son for three years from this coming Michaelmas, a yearly sum of four hundred dollars, with which to go to Goettingen and there, under the guidance of the excellent teachers of that place, to finish the work begun by you.

It is a real pleasure to me to announce this favor of our Monarch to you, and I shall always be ready to furnish you aid and protection during the time of your son's academic studies.

You are granted a two months' leave of absence, until Michaelmas, in which to arrange your affairs. I have given at the Magdeburg Consistory the necessary notice of your resignation.

I return to you the papers which you have sent me, and assure you of my high respect.

G. A. COMTE DE WOLFRADT.

I can report my son's progress as a university student in a few words: He continued everything which he had begun with me and attended lectures at Goettingen, in company with me. In the first semester I took up only two for him, ancient history with Heeren, and natural science with Mayer. I believed that in connection with the latter he would soon see the necessity for studying mathematics, as, in spite of all the preparation and repetition, there occurred occasions in the lectures when, on account of insufficient mathematical training, he was not able to understand something. After a lecture he once said to me, "I did not understand it,—I must study mathematics!" I provided for this at once. The excellent mathematician, Professor F., came that very evening and explained to him the difficult passage, and immediately started to give him a lesson in pure mathematics. My son and I will all our lives respectfully and gratefully remember this true friend.

It is well known that all the professors were very much satisfied with my son's industry and progress. I will, therefore, quote only a few of their testimonials, although I have the originals of them all:

The young K. Witte has this winter attended my lectures in ancient history and geography. I testify that he not only has diligently attended them in company with his father, but that I have also observed in him an attention which proceeded from his interest in the subject and a power of conception which is remarkable for his age. Would that these much promising aptitudes may be developed in their proper proportions.

A. H. L. HEEREN.

It gives me the greatest pleasure to testify to the fact that Mr. Karl Witte not only attended my lectures of natural science with unabated zeal and industry, but that he also has acquired such complete information in all the teachings of this science, as far as I have covered it in these lectures, that, after several examinations, I have become fully convinced of the ability which this hopeful youth has already shown in so many other trials of his skill.

J. T. MAYER.

The excellent condition of his health is proved by the fact that he did not fall ill that winter, for, instead of two or three hours, he had frequently to pass five and six hours in succession at his desk. Formerly he lived chiefly in the open, now he worked in the room. After six months of travel there followed six months of absolute rest. I did, indeed, take daily walks with him, but the winter was unusually rainy and stormy. Often we had to wander about in a terrible snow-storm, in order to get any exercise at all. On such days we used to be the only promenaders on the Rampart. "If I can bring him safely through the winter," I would say, "I shall have no further fear for his health." Thank Heaven, I succeeded in this.

As soon as the Easter vacation came, we both seized the wander-staff. That startled the people, for they expected that I would use the intermission in order to review the lectures with Karl and prepare him for the coming lectures, but especially in order to visit frequently the treasure of Goettingen, its library. Our friends were kind enough to recommend that to me, but they were also sensible enough to listen to my counter-reasons.

"If it were my purpose to make an exhibition of Karl, I would stay here. But I do not want to make a prodigy of him. I want to take care of his body, the expansion of his ideas, and the preservation of his good spirits. He will have time to learn a lot."

In the second semester Karl attended Schrader's lectures in botany and Thibaut's in mathematics. Here is the latter's testimonial:

Mr. Karl Witte has this last semester taken part in my lectures in pure mathematics, attending them with uninterrupted and exemplary diligence. Since I received him among my students not without anxiety, lest a continuous, abstract, scientific presentation should prove incompatible with his tender age, it is so much the more pleasant to me to be able to say that his lively interest in all the parts of the sciences presented, even the most difficult, has always remained the same. In the solution of the problems which were propounded in special hours for exercise he has yielded to no student. I may assert, in conformity with the strictest truth, that he has already given evidence of an excellent aptitude for mathematics.

B. FR. THIBAUT.

The collection of plants, the classification and preservation of them, gave him much exercise and pleasure. At the same time he drew, learned piano-playing and dancing, and carried on mechanical work. He continued his ancient and modern languages with me, in the philological seminars of Heyne, Mitcherlich, Wunderlich, and Dissen, and with Dr. Seebode, all the time we stayed in Goettingen. So I shall not mention this fact again, for everybody knows that these gentlemen were very much satisfied with him.

During that summer King Hieronymus came to Goettingen and, among other things, visited the Botanical Garden. My son was there with other students of botany. Leist noticed him and directed the king's attention to him. The king wanted to speak with him. Morio quickly picked him out of the crowd and presented him,—and soon afterward me also,—to both of the royal personages. The king conversed with us graciously for a long time, encouraged my son to further industry, and assured him, with this condition, of his constant, active protection. No sooner had this happened, than the first ladies and gentlemen of the court began to kiss the boy, as though he had become another person. Two generals led him between them, as in a triumph, until the king stepped into his carriage. Men from his entourage encouraged me now to ask for two or three hundred dollars of additional stipend, which would certainly not be refused. But I did not do so, because I preferred throughout my life to retrench my wants, rather than become troublesome by requests of money or offices.

In the third semester Karl took applied mathematics from Thibaut and natural history from Blumenbach, and, if I am not mistaken, it was that same winter that Mr. von

Seckendorf gave lectures on mimicry, which we also attended.

In the fourth semester, chemistry from Stromeier and, with Thibaut's express wish, mathematical analysis. Here follows the testimonial in regard to this science, which is very difficult for a boy not yet twelve years old.

Mr. Karl Witte in the summer semester of 1812 has attended my lectures on analysis and higher geometry. In spite of the considerable difficulties which the increase, both in volume and depth, in the investigation of these branches of theoretical mathematics inevitably brings with it, he has evinced the same continuous industry, the same constant attention as in his former study of the elements. Special examinations, based on these lectures, have afforded him additional opportunity to give conclusive proofs, excluding every doubt of the clearness, fluency, and thoroughness of the information acquired, as also of his ability to give a clever exposition of the same.

B. FR. THIBAUT.

In the fifth, Karl attended Mayer's lectures on goniometric instruments, Stronmeier's on reagents and the chemical apparatus, Hausmann's on mineralogical terminology and systematology, and Thibaut's on differential and integral calculus.

During this winter my son wrote his first

little work on higher mathematics. Thibaut had chosen the problem and had even concealed the name of the resulting curve so that Karl could not find any information about it. Yet the little work was everywhere received favorably. Many persons were particularly happy to get the instrument, invented and drawn by my son, for the mechanical drawing of the curve, because it proved most clearly his quickness of perception, his knowledge of mechanics, and his ability in representation.

In the sixth semester my son took practical geometry from Thibaut, theory of light and colors from Maier. French literature from Villers, and mineralogy from Hausmann. In the seventh semester he took political history from Heeren and reviewed ancient history with him.

During the previous summer Thibaut had declared to me that my son could learn nothing more of him. I had formerly wished that Karl might repeat some of his mathematical studies, but Thibaut insisted that he knew from the frequent tests that Karl had completely mastered his mathematics. I had also been opposed to his having studied the mathematical branches, especially the higher ones, in quick succession. I made strong remonstrances when my son in his eleventh year began analytics and higher geometry, and when he had to take up differential and integral calculus in his twelfth year. But Thibaut insisted that he possessed the necessary powers and sufficient desire for them, and "what a man likes to do, that is not difficult for him." I allowed him to do both with great anxiety, but with the two provisos (1) that he could stay away, if he found the subject too difficult, and (2) that he should be allowed to take a subject over, if he had not understood it perfectly. Thibaut agreed to this, with the jocular remark that there would be no need for it, in which he was right.

More important to me was his paternal advice to ask Gaus for private lectures for my son, which Gaus was to determine. Gaus knew Karl, but, at my request, he examined him again very carefully, after which he declared, "He cannot learn much more from lectures, not even from private lectures. But I will give him a series of Latin, Italian, and French authors, who have treated the higher branches of mathematics in the most profound manner. He can read them for himself!" I trembled, for Karl was only thirteen years old. "But, Professor," I said, "there is much which he will not understand!" "Much? No. Possibly a little, in which case I can help him. But he will not have occasion to ask often."

Gaus, too, was right. My son understood nearly everything. Cagnoli he grasped completely; the few passages, I believe there were three of them, in Poisson's "Higher Mechanics," which he found obscure Gaus found important enough to give him a written explanation of them. Even this great scholar has taken sympathetic interest in my son.

Although Karl no longer studied under Thibaut, the latter did not lose sight of him. "Let him do what he pleases," he once said to me, "I am curious to see what he will hit upon." I then revealed to him that my son was working on a plane trigonometry, but this was to be kept secret, because he was not yet sure whether time and circumstances would allow him to finish the work. Thibaut was very glad to hear this, saying, "Let him do what he pleases!" When the work was finished, he read it and approved the whole, but censured a few things, which Karl was gratefully anxious to correct. My son has, perhaps, never before worked with such joy, power, and endurance, as upon this self-imposed task.

The work appeared in 1815, when we were living at Heidelberg. To my astonishment I soon found a review of it by Thibaut, in which he evinced a totally different spirit than before. Instead of love there was hatred, instead of friendly censure harsh criticism, instead of a humane consideration for the author's youth (thirteen and a half years, which Thibaut purposely stated as "about sixteen") bitter, I may say, biting condemnation. Instead of representation of its clear meaning—malicious perversion of it. Thibaut has harmed us much by his onslaught, but we shall not forget his former love.

I received from His Majesty a continuation of the pension for four more years, with the gracious permission to use it wherever I found it expedient to be for the sake of my son. In order to obtain the arrears of the last seven months, we had to go to Brunswick, where we were introduced to the duke, although he was on the point of leaving. He spoke graciously to us for a long time. He tried to impress upon my son the desirability of going to England, where he would recommend him urgently to his relatives, in order that by their aid he might learn everything worth learning. The part of the money which was due in Brunswick was paid out to me that very day.

They were not less kind to me at Hanover, but, justly, wanted to have a proof of my son's knowledge. He had lately lectured to the seniors at Salzwedel on mathematics, and his lectures had there been received with great approval by the most excellent men. He offered to do something like it here, and merely asked for the themes. These were given to him from (1) algebra, (2) geometry, (3) analytics, (4) analytical trigonometry, (5) differential calculus, (6) integral calculus. He gave his lecture on the third of May, 1814, in the great auditorium of the Gymnasium.

The greatest scholars of the city were present. They knew that my son had received the themes on the previous day and that he had been out in society until late at night. He spoke with perfect ease, and yet so clearly and in such excellent German that several persons present walked back of the desk, because it seemed impossible to them that he should be able to speak so well without reading it off a paper. They smiled when they found they were mistaken. But my son, noticing their suspicion, left the desk and continued his lecture at the board, merely looking at his notes, in order to read off the themes. The applause was universal and enthusiastic. The Government sympathetically offered us a little more than was our due. The Duke of Cambridge assured us personally of his favor and recommendation if my son should go to England. Hessen, too, paid everything which I justly demanded; nay, the elector, like the Duke of Brunswick, asked me to state how much I was to get. We were several times invited to court, where we were showered with kindnesses.

In his eighth semester my son continued higher mathematics, philology, and so forth, and took logic from Schulze and analytical chemistry from Stromeier. Here is Stromeier's testimonial:

It gives me pleasure to certify to the fact that Mr. Karl Witte this summer semester not only attended my lectures on analytical chemistry and the practical exercises in the laboratory connected with these lectures with the same praiseworthy industry and zeal as were shown by him previously in my lectures on theoretical chemistry, but has also given me repeated proofs of his excellent knowledge of chemistry by the good execution of the chemical operations and analyses entrusted to him in the lectures, as well as by the elaboration of chemical subjects given him for home investigation.

DR. FR. STROMEIER.

During this semester we talked together regarding what he was to study in the future. If it had been my intention to make him famous in a brief time, I would have allowed him to continue to work in mathematical physics, chemistry, natural history, and mineralogy, for in all these sciences he was equally far advanced. But I was afraid that the deep investigations connected with these might not be good for his tender years. Moreover, if he proceeded on the path on which he had begun, he would have to become a professor, and that was not in conformity with my wish. So I decided that he should cultivate other fields of his mind, which heretofore had been lying fallow, and that later, in his eighteenth year, he should choose his vocation for himself. Accordingly I proposed diplomatics to him, where he would have to begin with law. His former studies had prepared him excellently for diplomatics, hence everybody agreed with me as to this plan. Only Thibaut, who formerly had urged me on to this move, now was sorry that his science was going to lose my son. "He can return to it later," I replied, "for he is still very young. If he is dissatisfied with law, he will certainly return to it."

During a journey to Wetzlar several members of the philosophical faculty at Giessen had a long and thorough conversation with my son. Then we were invited to dinner by the then Dean, the well-known Professor Schaumann, and here we found a select company. Suddenly all raised their glasses, drank my son's health, calling him "doctor noster," and the Dean, with a hearty embrace, handed him the following paper signed by himself. All persons present wept tears of joy.

"I. H. Fr. Carolo Witte, Doctori Nostro!

"My beloved young friend!

"Like all the public, I have long known of you. But it is only in these happy days that I have learned objectively how able you are, what you have become already. I have learned it with sincere joy. God has blessed the rare efforts of your worthy father. He is a father who rejoices in his son!

"My esteemed colleagues and I share this

paternal joy. We wish publicly to honor you, my friend, and your father through you.

"Hence I give you the official notice that the philosophical faculty yesterday voted unanimously to bestow the degree of doctor of philosophy upon you, and to send you the diploma as soon as it is printed.

"It gives me rare pleasure to be the first to call to you, 'Salve, doctor noster! Salve, salve, doctor carissime!'"

Here are the words of the diploma:

"To the youth, who is already a man by education, of amiable modesty,—in order at the same time to honor with the son the father, to whom the son owes everything, the degree and rights of doctor of philosophy, and so forth, to the honor of our university, etc., April 10, 1814."

In Marburg, Ullmann the elder and his colleagues were very happy at the honor conferred on Karl. Ullmann assured me that if it had not happened at Giessen, the University of Marburg would have given him the same degree.

CPSIA information can be obtained
at www.ICGtesting.com
Printed in the USA
LVHW082009220822
726594LV00005B/40

9 780343 314255